T Parentalk Guide to the Teenage Years

Steve Chalke

Illustrated by John Byrne

Hodder & Stoughton
LONDON   SYDNEY   AUCKLAND

British Library Cataloguing in Publication Data
A record for this book is available from the British Library

ISBN 0 340 72169 3

Typeset in Monotype Sabon by
Strathmore Publishing Services, London N7

Printed and bound in Great Britain by
Bookmarque Ltd, Croydon, Surrey

The paper and board used in this paperback are natural recyclable products
made from wood grown in sustainable forests. The manufacturing processes
conform to the environmental regulations of the country of origin.

Hodder and Stoughton
A division of Hodder Headline Ltd
338 Euston Road
London NW1 3BH

Part Three: Friends

FOREWORD

During his life, my husband Philip acted upon the premise that every young person can be a force for good. He believed, as I do, that our fundamental task as parents is to help them fulfil their unique potential.

This can be a difficult task, especially during the teenage years. It is a time when young people, in striving to forge new identities, are particularly susceptible to conflicting messages from society. Young lives can be thrown into turmoil. And, as parents, we are vulnerable too: our dreams of family harmony can, in reality, turn into nightmares!

So how refreshing it is to read *The Parentalk Guide to the Teenage Years*! Steve Chalke's approach is non-judgmental, providing practical ways to deal with many of the key issues that we face. It offers encouragement and positive guidance as we apply ourselves to this demanding, often daunting role.

It is also very humorous, reminding us that being a parent to a teenager is not just about dealing with problems but also about having fun!

Frances Lawrence
WEST LONDON, *October 1998*

PARENTING TEENAGERS IS A PROCESS OF TRIAL AND ERROR...
SURE IS - IF YOU THINK IT'S NOT GOING TO BE A TRIAL...
...YOU'VE MADE A BIG ERROR.

INTRODUCTION

Being a parent is, at one and the same time, the most wonderful privilege and the most daunting challenge of your life. This 'small task' will stretch you more than anything you've attempted before … and probably more than anything you'll ever face in the future. But for those who're willing to put in the effort, it can also be the most exciting, rewarding and fulfilling experience of your life!

If you're anything like me, there's a nagging feeling at the back of your mind that everyone else is doing a better job of being a parent than you are. But the truth is, they're not. We all make mistakes. None of us is perfect. We all do and say things that, with hindsight, we wish we hadn't.

In over fifteen years of dealing with family problems – both personally and professionally – I've come across very few parents who have any real confidence in their ability to do a good job. Though most mums and dads actually do an *excellent* job, they fall into the trap of measuring their performance against totally unrealistic 'ideals', and then feel inadequate when they can't match up.

The fact of the matter is, you'll never be a *perfect* parent. But not only can you be a good parent, you can even be a *great* parent – one your child is really proud of. And to achieve it, all you need are the three essential qualities available to every mum or dad whatever their situation in life: love, time and a little bit of self-trust.

Families aren't standard issue. They come in all shapes and sizes – not just the classic Hollywood version of mum, dad, two kids and a dog. There are models with one child and those with six – even those where all six were born together! There are those where the children, or some of them, have been adopted, and those where one is physically disabled or has a learning disability. And, for all sorts of reasons, there are those with just one parent – sometimes a mum, sometimes a dad. Sometimes there's a step-parent and step-children. But whatever your family looks like, this book is for you.

There are, of course, many reasons why you might be reading it: you may simply be looking for reassurance that what you're doing as a mum or dad is along the right lines; or you may need urgent help. Perhaps your child is in some kind of trouble, and you want to know what to do about it.

This book is about the basic principles and skills that every parent, regardless of their individual circumstances, needs in order not only to *survive* being a parent, but to *thrive*. But be warned: they're *not* short-cuts. They all require effort. The reason for this is simple: short-cuts just don't work.

So read on, because the relationship that any child has with their parent is the most formative and influential one of their lives. That's why my hope and sincere prayer is that this book serves you well.

PART ONE: HOME

Living with a Nocturnal Mammal

How Can I Survive Life with a Teenager?

The bedroom door creaks open just enough for Gary to make certain the coast is clear. He creeps out of his room and down the stairs as quickly as possible. His goal is simple: to slip out of the house without being ambushed by his mum. But despite his efforts, she still manages to accost him as he scuttles across the kitchen floor.

'Hi Gary!' she calls. 'You're up early.'

'Urgh,' he replies. More of a grunt than a recognisable word, but roughly translated into English, Gary's mum has learnt that it means 'Yes'.

'Where are you off to?' she asks, trying hard not to sound like the Spanish Inquisition. There's a forced smile on her face and an equally false (though expertly achieved) laid-back tone in her voice.

'Urgh,' Gary grunts again. His mum isn't quite sure, but she thinks that this 'urgh' is subtly different from the last one, meaning, 'Thanks for asking, mum. I'm going to John's for lunch, and then we're meeting Rob in town and all going on to the cinema.' She can't be entirely sure, however – she's new to learning Urghish, and still sometimes gets the grunts mixed up. They can all sound the same to an amateur.

'That'll be nice. When will you be back?' The same forced smile and happy-go-lucky tone.

This time, there's a particularly encouraging response: 'Urgh, urgh.' And with that, Gary picks up his coat and makes his way out of the back door.

'Bye then,' his mum calls after him. 'Have a good time. Don't be back too late!' In the distance, she can just make out another 'urgh' as Gary bounds down the road, without even turning his head to look back.

Something strange happens to a child when they enter the teenage years. Before your very eyes, they mutate – transformed from the naughty-but-cuddly child you used to know and understand into something far more worrying. Your child has entered … the Adolescent Zone. It's all rather bewildering.

When Charles Darwin stepped off the HMS *Beagle* in 1836 and began working on his now well-known theory of evolution, a lot of people thought he'd gone mad. But today, countless parents would be only too happy to offer their teenage son or daughter as indisputable proof that evolution is true. They're convinced that they have Neanderthal Man – the 'Missing Link' – living right under their roof. Not only do they look weird, they stomp around the house and they have a one-grunt vocabulary. What more evidence could anyone need?

Not every tumbling tot turns into a teenage tearaway, but every child – almost without exception – becomes more moody or withdrawn as they enter adolescence. The boy or girl you once couldn't prise off your leg – who always wanted you to kiss them better and tuck them into bed, and who never stopped talking – now seems to be allergic to conversations with you and is acutely embarrassed even to be seen with you in public.

It's all perfectly normal, but most parents still naturally wonder if they've done something terribly wrong, or accidentally become the worst parent in the whole world. Don't worry: you haven't.

ANY CHANCE YOU COULD BE JUST A LITTLE LESS WITHDRAWN?

Top Tip: *Don't worry if your teenager becomes withdrawn – it's normal.*

Ever since the Dawn of Man ...

You're not alone. Every parent since the beginning of time has travelled the same road.

> The world is going through troubled times. Today's young people only think of themselves. They've got no respect for parents or old people. They've got no time for rules or regulations. To hear them talk, you'd think they knew everything. And what we think of as wise, they just see as foolish. As for the girls, they don't speak, act or dress with any kind of modesty or feminine grace.

Sound familiar? Well that's what Peter the Monk had to say about it way back in AD 1274!

The transformation of your child into the creature from the blue lagoon won't necessarily coincide with the moment they enter the teenage years. The 'problem', as much as anything, is hormonal, and hormones kick in at different times for different kids – any time between the ages of twelve (sometimes even younger) and sixteen.

It's hard to generalise about what the impact of all this will be on any one child. Some become moody and rebellious, whilst others just go through a quiet or withdrawn phase. What you *can* guarantee is that, along with their mood swings, their taste in everything from music, clothes and food to friends, leisure activities and even parents will change. You'll shift almost instantaneously in their estimation from being leading contender for the title of 'Hero of the Universe' to outright winner of the 'Most Embarrassing Adult To Be Seen With' Award.

But if all this is hard for you to cope with, try to remember that it's even more bewildering for them. At least *you've* got the benefit of being older, wiser and more confident. And, though you can't expect them to believe it, you've experienced the same bewildering hormonal changes they're going through now – even if it *was* back in the days when dinosaurs ruled the earth!

> **Top Tip:** You're not alone. Every parent goes through it!

A Safe Port in a Storm

Change is frightening. We all love stability. So when puberty hits, like a violent storm, the result is chaos. It's as though someone has suddenly pulled up your anchor and left you fighting for survival, tossed back and forth on a ship you're not even sure how to control, let alone navigate safely.

And that's just how *you're* feeling! Imagine what your teenage son or daughter is going through! They've left the safe harbour of childhood and begun their journey to the distant land of adult life. But in the meantime, they're all at sea, with no previous experience to fall back on!

Childhood is just like a harbour. Inside its walls, your child is protected from life's extremes. They can enjoy calm waters – never too deep, too choppy or too far from dry land. All the important decisions are taken for them by you: what they wear, where they go, what they can do, etc. They're slowly learning the skills they'll need later on – how to steer and navigate, when to batten down the hatches and how to ride out the storms, etc. – but all within a safe, enclosed environment where help is always on hand.

Then, as they grow older, they start to hear fascinating stories about the distant land of adult privilege. Not only does it all sound exciting, but more importantly there's an inbuilt and irresistible compulsion in every teenager to leave the safety of the harbour, head for the open sea and feel the wind on their face. But the harsh reality is that they're headed for uncharted oceans in a vessel that's never before had to face the test of the elements. On their journey, they'll have to negotiate difficult, unpredictable and extreme conditions: one day they'll be buffeted by huge winds, the next they won't seem to be going anywhere. And it'll often take all the concentration they've got just to stay afloat.

So when your teenager is struggling a little to stay on course, resist the temptation to assume that you must have failed as a parent, and that you've got to air-lift them back to harbour as soon as possible in order to protect them from life's ups and downs. They may not fully have mastered the helm yet, but the last thing they need is for you to snatch the wheel back from them.

 Top Tip: Remember – your child is learning to fend for themselves.

The Life Cycle

Have you heard the one about the two young caterpillars watching a butterfly? One turns to the other and says, 'You'd never catch *me* up there in one of those contraptions!' It may not be flattering, but the truth is that adolescence is like the 'in-between' stage when a caterpillar finally decides they're ready to fly after all, and starts to prepare for the 'metamorphosis' needed to achieve their goal.

Teenagers are in-betweeners, at the awkward stage between childhood and adulthood. In fact, that's exactly how the *Oxford English Dictionary* defines the word 'adolescent': 'between childhood and adulthood'. They're no longer children, but they've not yet finished the 'metamorphosis' into mature adults.

However, unlike butterflies, teenagers don't cocoon themselves away from the world while they're metamorphosing – though sometimes *you* may be tempted to wish they would! Instead, they go through monumental changes in appearance and identity in full view of the rest of the world. And although puberty may not be the most concentrated or dramatic period of growth in a child's development, it's definitely the most difficult.

 Top Tip: *Be understanding – the teenage years are a real transformation.*

A Spot of Bother

So what makes adolescence so difficult? What is it that triggers the huge physical and emotional changes of the teenage years? You don't need to look any further for the culprit than *hormones*: the millions of little biochemical messengers that run riot in the body on instruction from the brain. It's your teenager's hormones that tell individual parts of their body to change from child to adult. Some trigger permanent changes, like growth spurts. Others regulate how the body works on a day-to-day, week-to-week and month-to-month basis. Oestrogen, for example, is the female hormone that controls a woman's reproductive cycle, instructing her ovaries to release an egg into the fallopian tubes every month.

Puberty begins for most girls between the ages of about eleven and twelve, though it *can* be earlier or later. Their breasts start to grow, which is sometimes painful. At the same time, they start to develop pubic and under-arm hair. All this can make them feel very awkward and self-conscious. Shortly afterwards – though again, the timing can vary considerably – they begin menstruation. No matter how well you've tried to prepare your daughter for the onset of periods, this can still be an immensely difficult time. Along with the development of breasts and curvy hips, it marks the end of childhood and the beginning of womanhood.

At this age, being average is everything. Not only are girls acutely aware of their own body changes, they're also aware of how these compare with those of their friends. If you're the first to develop, you're laughed at; if you're the last, still wearing vests or crop tops when all your friends are strapping on bras, you're equally prone to ridicule. Similarly, if your breasts are bigger than everyone else's, or smaller than everyone else's, it can make you feel like a bit of a freak. The only insurance against embarrassment is if everyone else is going through *exactly* the same changes at the same pace, maintaining the same standard measurements – and, of course, that never happens.

Boys develop on average a year or so later than girls, at least in terms of visible changes. They begin to grow taller and more muscular, and start growing facial and pubic hair. Their voice drops, as do their testicles, and they enter the bewildering world of erections and ejaculations. And just like girls, their skin often comes under sudden attack from spots, which erupt like Mount Etna all over their face.

But as if Total Body Transformation weren't enough to contend with, these physical changes are dwarfed by the emotional impact puberty can have. From hormone-induced anxiety or depression to the general teenage battle with self-esteem – 'Who am I? Does anyone like me? Am I ugly? Where do I fit in?' – adolescence can be a very rough voyage.

In the midst of this sea of turmoil and confusion, it's your job as a parent to act as an anchor. Always remember that, however bewildering the teenage years are for you, they're *much* worse for your child. What they need from you most is love, understanding and heaps of patience. They need you to be dependable – even though they can't be, and sometimes even *know* they can't be. *Something* in their life has to be immune to change, and as their parent – someone who loves them unconditionally – your role as a stable and reliable adult is essential. You may think they treat you like a fossil – they may even think of you as a fossil – but actually you're a rock.

 Top Tip: Be strong – you're the stable force in your child's life.

Neither One Thing nor the Other

In the film *My Fair Lady*, former flower girl Eliza Doolittle complains about the lack of respect her teacher, Professor Higgins, has for her. 'I shall always be a flower girl to Professor Higgins, because he *treats* me like a flower girl and always has. But I shall always be a lady to the Colonel, because he *treats* me like a lady and always has.'

How often have you heard a frustrated mum or dad ordering their child to 'act your age'? The truth is, of course, that their teenager *is* acting their age. *That's* the problem! What that parent really means is, 'Act older than your age. Act like me!' But children don't become instant adults when puberty strikes; instead, they mature slowly.

In the film *Big*, thirteen-year-old Josh Baskin makes a wish to become instantly big. The next morning, he wakes up to find that he's got the body of a thirty-year-old. But though he manages to find a job and a decent place to live, he's scared and bewildered, because he's inexperienced and immature. It's hardly surprising, really. After all, appearances can be deceptive. Whatever he may look like, underneath it all he *is* only thirteen years old.

Just like everyone else who ever walked the planet, including you, your teenager will need lots of encouragement if they're going to learn to behave confidently as an adult. If you think learning to play the guitar, or programme the VCR, or log on to collect your e-mail is hard, forget it – they're nothing compared to the effort and energy it takes to learn to behave like an adult.

So don't be surprised when your teenager still acts like a child. But however they behave, treat them like an adult from the moment they hit puberty. Rather than criticising and putting them down when they behave childishly, make sure you praise them and let them know you're proud of them when they behave responsibly. The more you *treat* your teenager like an adult, the more incentive you give them to *act* like one.

 Top Tip: *Always treat your child like an adult, but still expect them to behave like a child.*

13

Simon Says ...

A few years ago, I met an old man called Albert. He complained that he just couldn't understand 'today's young people'. 'When I was fifteen,' he told me, 'all I wanted to be was like my dad. I even wanted a suit like his.' Albert had looked up to his father. He'd respected him enormously. He couldn't think of anything better than to be just like him – even down to his taste in clothing.

Times have certainly changed. When I was fifteen, growing up in South London, the *last* thing I wanted was a suit – or any other piece of clothing – even remotely resembling my dad's. It's not that I didn't love him. I just wanted to be my 'own man'. (And besides, he had lousy taste in suits!)

In the first years of their lives, your kids actively *want* to copy what you do and say. You're their hero, and they want to be like you. Nothing matters to them more than what you think. You're their role model. They copy your words and actions. They even love dressing up in your clothes, pretending to be you though they're a fraction of your size. It's a vital part of growing up and learning. But they grow to become like you in more than just their appearance. For the most part, your values are their values. Your tastes become their tastes.

But as they enter Teen World, everything changes. Instead of wanting to be like you, in many ways their goal is to be as *un*like you as possible. In fact, they're often embarrassed just to be seen walking down the street with you, in case they should run into any of their friends. 'You're *not* going out in public dressed like *that*!' is as likely to come from their lips as it is from yours.

As adolescence kicks in, your teenager becomes more vulerable to the bombardment of messages hitting them through the media every day of their lives: look different, act different, talk different, walk different, dress different, think different, _be_ different. In some parts of the world, the oldest people in the village are still the most respected and most influential people around. But in today's Western world, what counts is what's fresh and new. To be young is to be the best. To be old is to be obsolete. One national newspaper headline I saw even claimed that, 'The only sin left in the UK today is to be old ... and get found out!'

So don't be surprised when your teenager gradually stops being who _you_ are and starts trying to find out who _they_ are. They'll stop wearing the clothes you picked out for them and start experimenting with their own style. And they'll stop believing all the things you taught them and start experimenting with their own values and views, reassessing things they've taken for granted until now.

 Top Tip: _Be patient – your teenager has a lot to sort through – but they'll get there._

'Do You Love It? Then I Hate It!'

Teenagers often question, or even appear to turn their back on, the values they've grown up with for no other reason than because they've grown up with them. They reject your values or contradict your opinions, not because there's anything wrong with them, but just because they're *yours*!

When younger children do the opposite of what you tell them, it's usually to test the boundaries you've set them and find out how serious you are about enforcing the rules. They *like* to know there are limits. It proves you care. It lets them know you're looking out for them. But with teenagers it's different. They're not doing the opposite of what you tell them in order to test *you* so much as to test *themselves*. The first step in finding out who they are is establishing that they're not *you*.

All this is part of learning to handle responsibility. For the first years of their lives, you've made all the major decisions for your child. But during adolescence, they start to become more independent, and they increasingly want to think and make decisions for themselves. Things they never thought twice about before suddenly become a real source of worry and concern. They know their decisions count for something, so they start thinking things through a lot more carefully.

In fact, even the *way* they think changes. Rather than accepting simple answers and explanations, they're beginning to realise how hard it is to make good choices. This is all part of accepting responsibility for their lives and their actions. And more often than not, the first step in making up their own mind about something is questioning what you've brought them up to believe. If you refuse to let them do this, you'll simply risk stunting their emotional and intellectual growth.

So try not to take their apparent rejection personally, even if your teenage son or daughter sometimes makes it seem *very* personal. 'You just don't understand' must be one of the most well-worn sayings in the teenage phrase book. And the way it's said usually leaves you in no doubt they think you're well past your sell-by date. But don't rise to the bait and they'll be back.

 Top Tip: *Don't take it personally – your child isn't so much rejecting* **you** *as finding* **themselves**.

Coming Around Again

'When I was a boy of fourteen,' Mark Twain famously commented, 'my father was so ignorant, I could hardly stand to have the old man around. But when I got to be twenty-one, I was amazed at how much he had learnt in seven years.' Try to remember when you were fourteen. What did it feel like? What did you enjoy the most? What frustrated you the most? What did you think of *your* parents? Do you still feel the same way?

In the film *Three Men and a Baby*, flatmates Peter, Jack and Michael are left to take care of Jack's baby daughter from a past relationship. At her wits' end, the baby's mum doesn't feel she can cope any longer with being a single parent. Initially, all the men can think of is how demanding little Mary is. She needs round-the-clock love and attention, which means they have to put their busy social lives and high-flying careers on hold. So they're all very relieved when Mary's mum comes back to reclaim her after a few weeks. But when everything in the flat has returned to normal, they start missing her. None of them realises just how much they've grown to love her until she's not there any more.

Peter, Jack and Michael needed to have a little bit of distance put between them and Mary before they could realise how important she'd become to them. And in exactly the same way, your teenager may well need to put some distance temporarily between them and the values you've taught them before they wake up to how *valu*able they really are.

But remember: the chances are, it's only a 'passing phase'. In time, they'll probably return to the values you instilled in them. But by then it'll be because *they* believe them, not because *you* do. They just need time to think them through and realise that they're values worth having. As the saying goes, 'You never know what you've got till it's gone.'

Top Tip: *Don't imagine your efforts have been wasted – they'll appreciate them in the long run.*

'You're not Going Out in That!'

<u>Which Battles Should I Fight to Win the War?</u>

'He who fights and runs away, lives to fight another day' – the rhyme originally composed by the American army at the Battle of Bunker Hill in 1775. After fighting the bloodiest battle in the whole War of Independence, the US Army was defeated. But Bunker Hill was a hollow victory for the British, who sustained terrible casualties over what turned out to be a fairly insignificant piece of land. Though they won the battle, they paid too high a price for it, and finally lost the war.

Family life has a way of catching you off guard. Its intensity gets under your skin and you end up losing your cool over all the wrong things. Minor incidents become full-scale dramas. With the benefit of hindsight, you realise they weren't that important in the first place. Your fourteen-year-old daughter wants to get her nose pierced or a tongue stud put in. Your fifteen-year-old son comes home with one side of his hair dyed green and the other side dyed pink – or worse, completely bald! You may not think it's elegant. It may not *be* elegant. But the truth is that it really doesn't matter that much in the grand scale of things.

So think about how any issue fits into the context of your on-going relationship with your son or daughter before wading in with both feet. Don't fight pitched battles over things that aren't really worth going to war over. Choose your battles carefully, or end up losing the war.

If your child's normal, there'll never be any shortage of important battles to fight and real issues to deal with. That's why it's vital not to get drawn into endless minor conflicts that don't really make any difference in the long run. Save your energy instead for the battles that count.

 Top Tip: Before you fight a battle, make sure it's worth it.

Cry Wolf

Not only will going to war over minor issues exhaust *you*, it'll also exhaust your child's respect for your judgment. They'll stop taking you seriously, and you'll end up like the boy who cried wolf too often when there was no wolf in sight. Slowly but surely, their trust in you will be eroded and destroyed, along with their ability to be honest with you.

If you make a big deal over something that doesn't really matter in the long run, how is your child meant to know when things *do* matter? If you overreact when they do something relatively insignificant, how are they supposed to know when they've really overstepped the line and done something that could have major repercussions? If you bring out your big guns over body-piercing, for example, what have you got in reserve for serious moral issues such as drugs, sex, alcohol, stealing, truancy, honesty or commitment?

By choosing your battles carefully, rather than allowing your home life to degenerate into a permanent war zone, you get to save your heavy artillery for the issues that really matter. That way, when you do dig your heels in and fight, your child will know that you're not kidding. It's not a false alarm. And since they know you care, they'll sit up and take notice.

What's more, if you fly off the handle at what seems to be the slightest provocation, they'll slowly become more and more immune to your anger or concern anyway. I used to live so close to a railway line that you could hear the trains whenever they rattled past, day and night – in fact, our windows would shake as they passed. After a while, I became used to the noise, and eventually I didn't even notice it any more. I effectively tuned it out. As a result, I was always surprised when friends came to stay and complained that the trains kept them awake at night. In just the same way, a parent who fights too many pitched battles will slowly find that their teenager becomes immune to their noise, learning to tune them out as effectively as I did the trains.

In Steven Spielberg's film *Hook*, Peter Panning's relationship with his twelve-year-old son is strained. Too many broken promises and meaningless disputes have stretched it to breaking point. So when Jack is kidnapped by the evil Captain Hook and taken to Never Never Land, Peter finds he's got not one but two battles on his hands. Not only does he have to fight Hook, but more crucially he also has to persuade Jack that it's *worth* coming back home. Before he can rescue him, Peter has to mend his relationship with his son, who has slowly tuned his father out of his life.

Your authority as a parent is based entirely on the strength of your relationship with your child. If they love and trust you, and know that you love and trust them, they'll often do what you ask even if they don't *really* want to. But if they don't, and they can possibly avoid it, they won't. So the more your child learns to tune you out, the harder you'll find it to get through to them about anything important.

Top Tip: Don't fly off the handle at every little thing, or you'll ruin your relationship with your teenager.

'You are Now Entering ... the Monosyllabic Zone'

Most of the battles you'll fight with your teenage child are actually the result of bad communication. Your child has entered the 'Monosyllabic Zone', where every question is answered with a grunt, or by muttering a single word under their breath if they're in a particularly talkative mood. This can be very frustrating.

When your child was younger, they insisted on telling you about everything they'd done – usually several times over, and very loudly. But as they enter the teenage years, they often sever the lines of communication. As they slowly become more independent, so they begin to rely more on other people and less on you for all their needs. And just as you did at their age, they'll start confiding more in their close friends than in you as their mum or dad. They'll gradually find other people their own age with whom to share the kind of small talk they used to share with you. You've been their closest and most trusted advisor over the years, and they still need your wisdom and guidance – it's just that they also need their own space.

WE'D LIKE A WORD WITH YOU ... OR TWO WORDS OUT OF YOU, WHICHEVER IS EASIER.

You may feel hurt at being effectively shut out of your child's life. But, believe it or not, it's a lot tougher for them. Becoming a teenager is a difficult stage in life, and one that even the happiest and most well-adjusted childhood can't totally prepare them for. It can be a lonely and isolating experience. That's why, although everyone wants to be young, no one ever wants to be fourteen again – they remember all too well how tough it was the first time around!

Of course, once the lines of communication start breaking down, it becomes harder to know what's going on in your teenage son or daughter's life. Just when you *need* to know what they're thinking – because you can't guess anymore – they stop telling you. So try not to jump to conclusions. Don't mistake their reluctance to communicate for outright rebellion. At the same time, don't try to overcompensate. If you're not careful, they'll misinterpret your healthy interest in what they're doing as a smothering form of 'third degree' interrogation.

For instance, when your teenager ignores your repeated requests to clean their room, don't automatically assume they're being deliberately disobedient and unhelpful. They may well be preoccupied and distracted by other things that're going on in their life. So back off a bit, and give them the space they need. Don't wade in with all guns blazing. Try to keep things in perspective. After all, the world is full of wise, mature, honest, generous, wonderful people who just happen to be untidy – it's not that big a deal! Only draw a line in the sand when you're really sure that it has to be there. Otherwise, not only will your child be tempted to shut you out altogether, they'll also be deprived of your help, support, love and advice on the things that matter when they desperately need it.

LOOK, I THINK TEENAGERS NEED PRIVACY TOO... BUT POSTING HIM TO SIBERIA IS MUCH TOO DRASTIC!

Top Tip: *Learn to give your teenager their own privacy and 'personal space'.*

Drawing a Line in the Sand

When it comes to teenagers, there are basically only two types of battle you'll ever have: those that really aren't worth fighting in the first place, and those you can't afford to lose. It's not easy, but it's your task as a responsible mum or dad to think through the long-term implications of your child's attitudes and actions, and to have the courage to draw a line in the sand when it really has to be there.

If you say 'No' over something but then back down (unless you were actually wrong to say 'No', in which case you'll need to apologise), you'll have sent your child the very clear message that you don't really mean what you say, and that if they stand up to you for long enough, they'll eventually get their own way. If they learn that they can turn a 'No' into a 'Yes' as long as they're persistent, and willing to raise the stakes high enough, they'll repeat the lesson over and over again. Ignoring you when you say 'No' – even over very serious things – will become a habit.

Rules and boundaries are there to teach teenagers to handle freedom within safe limits. If you don't let your child make their own decisions (and mistakes) within those limits, they'll never learn to handle freedom wisely when they're old enough to leave home. They'll grow up lacking the experience needed to make good decisions for themselves. As the saying goes, 'Good decisions come from experience, and experience is what we learn from making bad decisions!' On the other hand, if you give your child too much rope, they could end up hanging themselves with it. If you don't set safe limits and boundaries to teach them discipline, they'll never acquire the self-discipline they'll need if they're to make a success of their life and stay out of trouble!

Top Tip: *If a battle's worth fighting at all, you can't afford to lose it.*

Anything Goes?

I recently talked to a parent whose teenage son was totally out of control. His actions were no longer just embarrassing: they were now dangerous, both to himself and others.

'I can't understand it,' they told me. 'We gave him everything he wanted.'

Sadly, *that* was just the problem! My friend Rob Parsons tells the story of when he took his son to a basketball game. Knowing how short a six-year-old's attention span was, he laid out some ground rules to begin with. 'Now son,' he told him, 'you can run up and down the aisles and all round the stands, but you mustn't cross the thick white line where the players are. Do you understand?'

His son nodded obediently and they both settled down to wait for the game to start. But the moment the whistle blew, Rob's son got up, rushed down to the front of the stands, turned to look at his father – and deliberately put one foot over the white line. It's as if he was saying, 'Dad, I understand the rules perfectly. You've explained them very clearly. Now what are you going to do about it?'

Rob had to punish him. If boundaries aren't clear and enforced, children simply learn that breaking them is OK. And the more 'lines in the sand' they learn to kick over, the more difficult it becomes for them to accept any limits in the future.

In 1924 Chicago, university students Nathan Leopold and Richard Loeb killed a local schoolboy. Dubbed 'the crime of the century', the trial made headline news around the world because the young men had no motive for the killing. Rich, privileged and highly intelligent, they'd simply come to believe they were better than everyone else. They felt they were above the law, and could do what they liked – including murder.

Amazingly, they made no effort to hide their guilt. They even confessed. In their own minds, they simply hadn't done anything wrong. Not surprisingly, the judge disagreed. The only question to be settled was, should they be given the death penalty? Arguing in their defence, the most famous lawyer of his generation, Clarence Darrow, suggested that the two young men were 'emotionally immature'. Spoilt by their wealthy parents, he argued, they'd never learnt to respect the proper boundaries. The judge sentenced them to life in prison.

It may be an extreme example, but it shows what can happen when, rather than fighting *every* battle, parents decide not to fight *any* battles. Learning where the limits are is part of being human. If *you* don't teach your children the difference between *right* and *wrong* – and then enforce those limits – sooner or later someone else will! And it'll hurt a lot more if someone else has to do it than if you do.

> **Top Tip:** Not fighting **any** battles is as bad as fighting **every** battle!

A Word in Anger

They say that fanaticism consists of redoubling your efforts when you've forgotten your basic aim. In Shakespeare's play *Romeo and Juliet*, two families – the Montagues and Capulets – are at each other's throats. They've been at each other's throats for a long time. In fact, they've been at each other's throats for so long that no one can remember quite why they were at each other's throats in the first place. Somewhere back in the mists of time, things just got out of hand, and then stayed that way permanently.

Once a battle has started, the stakes can get very high, very quickly, especially if the argument touches a raw nerve. In the heat of an argument, both sides can end up saying things they don't really mean. And as a result, an already tense relationship can be made worse. So what can you do to make sure that you don't accidentally trigger off full-scale nuclear armageddon?

Why not take a leaf out of the American Football rules book and call for a 'time out'? If you feel your hackles start to rise, back out before you get carried away. Tell your teenage son or daughter that you're too angry to talk about things now, and find a quiet spot somewhere (or go for a walk) to get it out of your system and work out what the stakes really are before saying any more.

By giving yourself time to cool off and think things through, you can make sure that you're not reacting to your child out of vengeance or frustration with something or someone else, or lashing out in the heat of the moment in a way you'll regret later. And if, after a bit of thought, you become convinced that this is a battle you really can't run away from but have to fight, you can calmly sort through how you're going to tackle the situation in order to win the day without losing the child.

Top Tip: *Taking 'time out' helps focus your thoughts and your energy.*

Making Up

How Can I Mend Relationships When It All Goes Wrong?

Michael was a high-flying businessman who'd built his own company up from scratch to become one of the most successful in its field. His work took him around the world, but success quickly went to his head. He was friends with the rich and famous, but at the cost of spending time with his wife and kids. His work and social life kept him away from home when they needed him most. Things went from bad to worse, and when he and his wife finally separated, Michael moved out altogether.

Then, at the age of forty six, Michael was diagnosed as having cancer. He was told he had just weeks to live. This tragic news brought him to his senses. He decided to spend as much time as he could with his children. But the problem was, they no longer trusted him and found it very hard even to be with him, let alone hold a relaxed conversation with him. They'd seen how much time he'd put into other things – things they knew mattered to him – and how little time he spent with them, and had long since reached the conclusion that he didn't love them. And from there it was only a short step to believing that he didn't love them because there was nothing about them *worth* loving.

The truth is, of course, that Michael loved his children very much. He'd just made some bad mistakes, which he'd never had the courage to deal with until it was too late. Given time, I'm sure Michael's children would slowly have learnt to trust him again. The problem was that time was the one thing Michael didn't have.

All children need their parents' love and time to enable them to mature into happy, self-confident people. When we allow other things – whatever they are – to get in the way of our relationship with them, we starve them of the emotional oxygen they need to develop into healthy, independent adults. So if you've fallen out with your teenager, make up your mind to put things right, and to start today.

 Top Tip: *Your teenager **needs** your time, so don't deprive them of it.*

The Miracle Cure?

None of us is perfect. However hard we try, we all make mistakes. So what do you do when it's all gone horribly wrong? You've let your teenage son or daughter down or lost your temper with them again. Or you've treated them in a way you're ashamed of, and relationships are 'icy' cold, to say the least. Where do you go from here? How do you make peace? How do you begin to rebuild the

31

bridges between you and your child? How do you start again?

The first thing to realise is that there *is* a way back. You *can* make amends, however bad things seem to have got. Obviously, a 'flashpoint' incident, where anger has flared up quickly over something specific, is going to be a lot easier to deal with than long-term relationship failure, where bitterness and resentment have been allowed to build up over many years. But strangely, it's exactly the same 'medicine' that's needed to treat both problems – all that's different is the recovery time.

The fact is, your relationship with your child has an amazing in-built capacity to heal itself. The reason for this is simple: they *want* to forgive you. They *want* to love you. They *want* to enjoy a good relationship with you. They need *your* love and respect more than you can ever possibly imagine – without it they're incomplete. And all this gives you a massive head start. It'll take time, of course. Perhaps even a long time. But the damage *can* be healed if you're willing to put in the effort.

Top Tip: *Your teenager **wants** to rebuild their relationship with you, so don't give up.*

Behind Closed Doors

As the saying goes, 'people always save their worst behaviour for the home'. Even the best parents in the world have weak spots. In fact, we often treat our families worse than we treat strangers. We spend so long being 'nice' to people outside the home that by the end of the day we're exhausted. Our patience has run out. So when our child annoys us, we lash out, unloading our pent-up anger and frustration on them. It's not their fault – they just happen to be in the wrong place at the wrong time, and we don't feel we've got the energy to be courteous or tolerant any more.

In business, Andrew was a real diplomat. Though he had strong views, his job – which involved dealing with people all over the world, from very different cultures – constantly required him to make the effort to be both tactful and charming. But when he got home, it was a different story. He was a good dad, and loved his kids very much. But he never showed them the same tact and courtesy he had to show others. He was never as patient, and far more stubborn. He rarely made the same effort at home as he did at work. After all, he thought, if he couldn't relax and be himself with his family, who *could* he relax and be himself with? They'd understand.

But whatever our excuse, whenever we take our family for granted, we're paving the way for eventual tension and division.

By saving our worst behaviour for home, we give our children the impression that they're not important enough to deserve better treatment. It's obvious, really. Our kids can't see our attitudes, emotions or good intentions – only our behaviour. So their understanding of how we feel about them is based solely on how we actually treat them.

We send our children mixed messages all the time. Some are good and some are bad. It'd be great to think that we were always in total control of the kind of signals we give out, but a lot of the time we're not. Even when we use all the right words, we can still upset people because of *how* we say them. If we've had a bad day, for instance, it'll usually show in the tone of our voice.

And it's not just how *we* say things. It's how we react to the things our kids say to us. If we're in a bad mood, we snap at them – not because of anything they've said, but just because they're unfortunate enough to have been in the wrong place at the wrong time. Occasionally an exhausted or exasperated parent will even trigger a bitter, and perhaps long-lasting, rift by overreacting to their teenager with such classic lines as, 'If you do that once more, you'll never show your face in this house again!', and then not having the courage to back down and apologise. The truth is that we all blow it from time to time, whoever we are – after all, we're only human!

 Top Tip: *Remember – no one's perfect. Every parent makes mistakes.*

'Sorry' Seems to be the Hardest Word

The good news is, you can turn a minus into a plus. You can make positive use of even your worst foul-ups.

We all want our children to be honest and brave enough to admit when they've made mistakes. If they've done something to hurt someone else, we want them to be big enough to own up, apologise and ask for forgiveness. But how can they possibly learn to do this if *we* never admit to *our* mistakes or apologise to them?

Some parents worry that apologising to, or asking for forgiveness from, their kids will be seen as a sign of weakness. They're concerned that any chink in their armour will be exploited. If they come across as 'weak', their teenager will lose respect for them. Others worry that by apologising for what they've said and done, they'll come across as excusing – or, worse still, even condoning – their teenager's behaviour or attitudes. But the truth is, it's the parents who never admit when they're in the wrong who eventually lose their child's respect.

Apologising when you've hurt someone isn't a sign of weakness. It's actually a sign of strength. It takes courage. Rather than under*mining* your authority, it under*lines* it. It sets a good example, encouraging your child to apologise when they've done something wrong themselves. It also builds trust and softens the atmosphere.

Learning to apologise is hard, of course, especially if you're feeling insecure and lacking in self-confidence. But that's just how any teenager feels when they're at the receiving end of your anger or insensitivity. They'll only begin to find the strength to admit their mistakes and ask forgiveness when they feel secure and unthreatened. So even if you think your teenager's attitude or behaviour has been completely out of line, by apologising for any harsh words or personal attacks you made when *you* reacted, you'll make it far easier for *them* to learn how to apologise for their mistakes and failings.

Top Tip: By apologising yourself, you help your teenager learn to apologise.

Getting the Habit

But there's another, more common reason why most of us don't apologise to our kids, and it's a lot simpler: we're just not in the habit.

It's very hard to say sorry. Our mistakes don't exactly show us in the best light, so we want to ignore or forget them, not focus on them. When we apologise, we have to face up to the fact that we're capable of hurting people – either from cruelty or carelessness. We also admit that we care about the people we've hurt, enough to feel bad and want to put things right. And this kind of emotional honesty – especially if we're not used to it – can be very embarrassing. That's why it's a habit most of us just don't have.

Nevertheless, learning how to apologise and ask for forgiveness when you've treated you teenager unfairly is a habit well worth working on, because:

- an apology can melt resentment and create respect, paving the way for forgiveness and reconciliation on both sides;
- an apology sets an example, helping your teenager build the confidence to admit when *they've* done wrong or hurt someone;
- an apology shows your teenager that they can admit their errors without losing face;
- an apology shows your teenager that failure isn't a kind of unforgivable sin, and it's OK to make mistakes – everyone does it, even you;
- an apology shows respect, telling your teenager that they're valuable to you and you care about how they think and feel.

Top Tip: *Apologising is a good habit to acquire.*

Crash Landing on Planet Earth

In fact, if you're prepared to admit to your failures and weaknesses, you can even use them to bring about something positive, making them part of the creative influence you have on your teenager. By admitting that *you* get things wrong too, you teach them that acknowledging failure and apologising are OK, and that failure itself is inevitable.

My friend Karen says that the best thing her dad ever did for her was crash the car! It's not that he was a bad father. In fact, if he hadn't been such a good dad, crashing the car would never have made such an impact on her. Karen's dad was kind and loving, and on top of that he seemed to have an almost encyclopaedic knowledge of virtually everything except pop music. But all this just made Karen aware of the huge mountain she had to climb to be like him.

And then, when she was fourteen, he crashed the car. No one was hurt, but Karen was never the same again. She'd seen the accident coming. Assuming that her dad had seen it coming too, she hadn't said anything. As the other car ploughed into the side of them, Karen's surprise quickly gave way to a realisation not only about her dad, but also about herself. By accidentally crashing the car, he hadn't just shown her that it was OK to make mistakes. Without knowing it, he'd also shown her that she saw things he didn't, and that he needed her just as much as she needed him.

For the first few years of their lives, you're a real hero to your child. But by the time they're a teenager, they're already starting to see your weaknesses for what they are. So rather than trying to hide them, why not use them to teach your teenager that it's OK to be 'only human'?

Top Tip: *Admitting your weaknesses can help your teenager discover their strengths.*

Making the First Move ...

Almost all of us have got some incident deeply etched into our memory of how, when we were a teenager, we felt unfairly treated by our parents. We all get hurt by others, but teenagers can often feel injustice or rejection particularly acutely and their memories are very long. So if you don't do all you can to sort out your problems and put things right as you go along, you'll just be storing up trouble further down the line. Time *can* be a great healer, but wounds are actually more likely to fester if they're not dealt with quickly.

It may not seem fair (in fact, it's often *not* fair!), but if things have gone wrong between you and your teenage son or daughter, it's your job as a parent to make the first move to put them right. If you've fallen out with each other, don't wait for *them* to apologise to you. It doesn't matter how much you think they were to blame for causing the problem in the first place – you're the parent, the mature adult, and they're not. They're still in training. So 'act your age' – it's *your* responsibility to hold out the olive branch.

- **If it was your fault,** begin by apologising. Say something like, 'I've had a bad day and I took it out on you. I shouldn't have. I'm sorry.' Or, 'I didn't mean to shout at you. I wish I'd never done it. I'm sorry.' Whatever you do, make sure your apology is *sincere*. It's all right to give reasons for your actions, but don't make lame excuses. Most of us are pretty good at twisting apologies so far round that in the end they become attacks: 'I'm sorry. I shouldn't have lashed out at you, but you were wrong to say what you did and you deserved it.' This kind of 'apology' is almost guaranteed to spark off another row, and make things even worse.

- **If you were *mostly* or *partly* to blame,** then bite the bullet. Admit to what *you* did wrong, and don't try to justify it. Most family fights are a case of 'six of one and half a dozen of another'. They may begin small, but they quickly escalate into something close to full-scale nuclear armageddon because no one wants to back down and admit they were wrong, even if they *know* they were. By making the first move, you'll make it easier for your teenager to admit their own mistakes. They're probably feeling bad about what they said or did. So if you give the lead, they may be able to admit they were wrong, and say sorry for their part in things. Even if they don't, you've still defused the situation and given them lots to think about and learn from.

- **If it wasn't your fault *at all*,** you still need to make the first move. But even if you're convinced there's no blame whatsoever on your side of the fence, *don't say so*! You'll only put your teenager on the defensive again, even if they were ready to apologise. It's an instinctive reaction to defend yourself when someone attacks you, so try to say something comforting and constructive instead: 'I guess your day was horrible. So was mine. But I really don't like arguing. Let's put this behind us.'

 Top Tip: *As the adult, it's your job to make the first move when it's all gone wrong.*

... And the Second, Third, Fourth and Fifth

Of course, the first move may not always work. Even if you bend over backwards to be forgiving – and set a new World Record for Humility – it still may not produce the kind of response you were hoping for. In fact, your kindness may go totally unnoticed.

Don't expect too much too soon. If you've been going through a hard patch, things won't improve overnight, so be prepared to stick at it. Your persistence will eventually pay off, slowly breaking down the resentment, pain or distrust that exists. Even if they show no immediate sign of positive response to you – or even recognition that you're trying – your patient attitude will tell your teenager that you do love them. It'll also send them the message that you respect them enough not ride a coach and horses through their emotional independence – even when they're acting completely selfishly!

By making the first move, you're building a bridge between you and your teenager. Believe it or not, underneath it all they want to get things sorted out as much as you do. But they don't have the knowledge, self-confidence or maturity to begin building bridges on their own. Remember: your teenager may look like an adult, and sometimes even act like an adult. But they're not all the way there yet. They're still an *adolescent*. So it's up to *you* to make the first move. It's your job to do all you can to re-establish an atmosphere of trust rather than hostility between you.

If your first steps toward peace haven't been as successful as you'd hoped, persevere. Remind yourself that your relationship with your teenager is more valuable than anything else in the world. If you're really serious about ending the rift between you, you'll have to make the *second* move as well as the first. And if that doesn't work, you'll have to make the *third* move, too. And the *fourth*. And the *fifth*. The secret to success is simply this: however often your overtures of peace are rejected, keep your cool and keep going. And whatever you do, don't lose your temper and shout – or you'll find yourself back at square one. If you start trying to cross the bridge you've just built with all guns blazing, don't be surprised when they blow it up again.

 Top Tip: *If at first you don't succeed in putting things right, try again!*

The Time to Act Is NOW!

When Brian and Joan fell out with their sixteen year-old son Philip, they made it clear that they wouldn't say another word to him until he apologised. And they haven't. The problem is, the falling out happened eighteen months ago! For eighteen crucial months, the three of them have lived in the same house, eaten the same meals and even shared some of the same friends. But the only communication Brian and Joan have had with their son is via notes stuck to the fridge! He doesn't speak to them and they don't speak to him. In other circumstances, it would be funny!

Everyone hates the situation, but for Brian and Joan it's a matter of principle. They're teaching Philip to accept responsibility for his words and actions. Until he admits he was wrong to say what he did, they just have to be 'strong and silent'. 'It'll work out right in the end,' Brian tells his friends. 'He'll come to his senses one of these days. You'll see.' But the truth is that Philip knew at the time that he was wrong to say what he did. That was the point – he'd *wanted* to upset them! Five minutes later, of course, he regretted it. But by then it was too late. Though he desperately wanted to apologise, he didn't know how. And the longer the situation has dragged on, the harder it's become.

It's always tragic to hear about family rows that have rumbled on for years, especially when parents and teenagers are no longer even on speaking terms as a result. Mums and dads refuse to have anything to do with their kids. Sons and daughters have no time for their parents. Sometimes the causes of a family feud are hidden so deep in the past that no one can really remember why they started in the first place, whilst in other cases, and with the power of hindsight, the initial reasons seem to be almost trivial.

But once a rift is in place, it doesn't matter how it came about.

Unless *both* sides are prepared to forgive, there'll never be a reconciliation. However, even though your teenager is on the crest of becoming an adult, you're still their parent. That means it's *still* your job to make the first move and be the first one to forgive and ask for forgiveness. This isn't a matter for debate: it goes with the territory.

The longer you put it off, the harder it gets. There's a great deal of common sense in an old saying from the Bible: 'Don't let the sun go down when you're still angry.' In other words, the quicker you settle a dispute, the less damage it'll do. So don't put off making the first move. Even if a dispute has been going on for a long time, do something to end it *today*! Start by deciding that rather than trying to apportion blame, you'll just forgive and be ready to ask for forgiveness.

Top Tip: *The longer you put it off, the harder it gets to build bridges.*

'Trouble at Mill!'

When negotiations break down between a company's workforce and its management, there's little to be gained if the two sides just stand on their soap boxes and trot out their well-rehearsed rhetoric. Progress can only be made when both sides are prepared to sit down and discuss the whole thing sensibly. There are important lessons to be learnt from the world of industrial relations, ones that apply equally to family life.

- Successful negotiations depend on both sides being **willing to listen.** It's amazing how much you can achieve just by listening to each other. In fact, *most* problems in the home are either caused or made worse by one side not listening to the other. We can be so busy with our own concerns that we don't pick up on our teenager's hurts and needs, and their legitimate grievances. Or else the atmosphere has become so hostile that, rather than listening to what they're saying, we use the time they spend talking to devise ways of knocking holes in their argument as soon as they pause for breath.

- Successful negotiations also depend on **compromise.** Sometimes, of course, this just isn't possible. We need to take a firm stand, because our teenager is in real danger of hurting themselves and others if they continue with what they're doing. But most of the time, all that really stands in the way of genuine compromise is pride. Many rows are caused by one side or the other digging their heels in and refusing to give way on something because it would hurt their pride. It's not a question of safety or discipline. They just don't want to give in. Once again, it's your job to make the first move and swallow your pride. Don't worry about compromise undermining your authority: compromise *isn't* surrender. Instead, like an apology, it'll show your child that you respect and understand their wishes. Compromise is two-sided, so you won't be the only one giving ground. It changes a conflict (win–lose) situation into one where both sides work together to find a win–win solution.

- In extreme cases, when both sides come to a stalemate, **arbitration** may be needed. This is where someone else – acceptable to both sides, with a more objective view of the situation – helps to achieve an agreement. The arbiter is there to help you listen to each other without going ballistic at what they say, enabling you to find a way forward. When nothing else works, you may need to rely on some form of arbitration to end a row. It could be your partner, another family member or a good friend. Or you could get help from a professional counsellor. As always, it's up to you to suggest it, and so show willing to give ground.

Top Tip: Relationships are always give and take, so don't be afraid of compromise.

PART TWO: SCHOOL

Decisions, Decisions ...

How Do I Help My Teenager Make Career Choices?

When Richard Branson was in the last years of school, his dad became extremely concerned about his academic progress – or, to be more accurate, the lack of it. Richard excelled at sport, but that was about it. So one day Mr Branson Senior decided to take his son for a walk. He explained to him how vital it was to have something to fall back on, and urged him to work hard to become a lawyer. The adolescent Richard made lots of positive noises, and his dad went home very pleased with the way the conversation had gone.

But the next day, Mr Branson began having second thoughts. Overnight, he'd recalled how much he hated it when *his* dad had given him the same speech years before. So the following weekend, he took his son for another walk. This time he told Richard to ignore the previous advice and instead do whatever he wanted with his life. Judging by his success, the multimillionaire boss of the Virgin Group of companies took his dad's second piece of advice to heart. The rest is history.

Of course, not *every* child will 'reach the top' in their chosen profession. But *every* parent can learn the vital lesson Richard Branson's father learnt. Rather than trying to enforce our *own* dreams and expectations on our teenagers – perhaps ones we never managed to live out ourselves – our responsibility is to help them realise *their* dreams and expectations.

I ALWAYS GIVE YOU A CHOICE. DO WHAT I SAY, OR BE MADE TO DO WHAT I SAY.

It's a key part of your job as a parent to help plan your son or daughter's life *with* them, but never try to plan it *for* them. Quite apart from anything else, telling any teenager they *have* to do something is an almost cast-iron method of ensuring they *won't* do it, just as telling them *not* to do it is a guaranteed way of ensuring they *do*! As Monta Crane put it, 'There are three ways to get something done: do it yourself, hire someone, or forbid your kids to do it!'

Top Tip: *Help your teenager make their **own** choices – don't make them for them.*

'A Guitar's All Right, Son ...'

When International Business Machines first heard about the idea of a personal computer, they dismissed it as a gimmick. 'No one will ever be interested in a personal computing machine,' a spokesperson claimed. They gave it the official thumbs down and decided to stick with the good old typewriter. At the time, computers were the size of large rooms, and only big institutions and companies could afford them. However, just a few years later, IBM realised their mistake and today are better known for their PCs than anything else.

History is filled with men and women who achieved what others were convinced was impossible, armed with little more than *vision*. That fact alone should make us wary of trying to dictate to our child what they can or can't, should or shouldn't do with their life.

In the late 1950s, almost every teenage boy in Liverpool seemed to be a member of a 'skiffle' band. Musical talent was optional in these makeshift groups, where instruments such as washboards and one-string double basses were as common as guitars and drums. Mimi Smith was worried that her nephew was taking all this music-making business too seriously. Having raised him as a son, she wanted the best for him. She begged him to concentrate

49

more on his schoolwork and less on playing the guitar. 'A guitar's all right, John,' she told him, 'but you'll never earn your living by it.' How wrong she was! By 1966, his band – the Beatles – was so famous that John, Paul, George and Ringo had become legends in their own lifetimes. And ever since, billions of people around the world have been glad that John Lennon didn't listen to his Aunt Mimi.

It's not your job as a parent to tell your teenage son or daughter what they *can't* do with their lives. They get plenty of that from the rest of society. What they need from you most is encouragement and support, not criticism. It's your task to help them see what they *can* do – the things they *can* achieve if they put their mind to it. A wise mum or dad is one who gives their teenager enough space to work their own ambitions out for themselves, whilst at the same time being 'open all hours' to chat things over, helping them assess the various possibilities when they need to.

Don't let *your* fears get in the way of *their* dreams. The truth is, the more we criticise and put down our teenagers' ideas, the harder we make it for them to achieve anything at all with their lives. We may convince ourselves that all we're doing is introducing a much-needed dose of reality into their pipe dreams, cutting them down to size, but more often than not what we're actually doing is creating a kind of negative 'self-fulfilling prophecy'. By dismissing their dreams as 'impossible', we either drive a wedge into our relationship with them and force them to rebel against our judgment, or we *make* their ambitions unattainable by forcing them to accept our defeatest assessment of their situation.

Top Tip: *Don't tell your teenager what they can't do. Help them to work out what they can.*

Silence is Golden?

It's said that if you give a good idea to an American, by the time you've finished explaining it to them they'll give you three reasons why it's the best idea they've ever heard. But if you give the same idea to a Brit, by the time you've finished they'll have come up with three reasons why it'll never work even in a month of Sundays! It's too easy to criticise, rather than give positive guidance, support and encouragement.

How often have you heard someone say things like, 'They don't really appreciate me' or, 'My boss just doesn't value me'? I hear this all the time. The funny thing is, in most cases I *know* it isn't true – often because their friends, colleagues or bosses have *told* me it isn't true. Sadly, the same friends, colleagues and bosses have never told the person in question. So all *they* ever hear is what's wrong with them.

I once heard about a couple whose marriage was about to collapse after fifteen years. A friend arranged for them to see a professional counsellor, more or less frogmarching them to the door. Neither of them wanted to break up, but living together had become intolerable. When the counsellor asked them both what they thought was the root of the problem, the wife said, 'It's simple. He doesn't love me any more.'

51

'That's ridiculous,' the husband replied. 'She *knows* I love her.'

'What makes you say he doesn't love you?' the counsellor asked the wife.

'He never tells me he loves me.'

'That's not true,' the husband piped up indignantly. 'I told her I loved her on our wedding day, and I said I'd let her know if I ever changed my mind!'

The truth is, all of us imagine that people who never *tell* us they appreciate us, *don't* appreciate us. Our children are no different. We assume they *know* we love them, and *know* what's good about them, but we never actually *tell* them. When they're smaller, of course, we often tell our children we love them. But as they get older, its easy to stop, taking it for granted they know by now! They don't! What's more, they're quite likely to reach the conclusion that we don't *tell* them we love them any more because we *don't* love them any more.

Underneath a brash exterior, your teenager's confidence is brittle and easily shattered. Silence, or a few insensitive and discouraging words from you, can have a devastating impact on their self-esteem, leaving them emotionally crippled for years to come. At the very least, it will act as a big dampener on their enthusiasm.

When I was at college, part of my course involved trying to master the art of public speaking. Twice a week a student was chosen to give a talk in front of the tutors and other students, who were expected to listen and then pinpoint every mistake. The exercise was designed to help us improve our skills by exposing us to some 'healthy criticism'. But more often than not it had precisely the opposite effect. The problem was that people only ever said what was *wrong* with a talk; they never thought of giving anything like the same kind of attention to what was *right* with it. They just assumed that what was good didn't need explaining. But those of us who nervously had to give the talks usually came to a different conclusion: nothing positive had been said because there wasn't anything positive to say. The few small drops of positive feedback there were got drowned in the vast ocean of negative criticism.

THE CRITICISM I HAVE OF YOU SON IS THAT YOU'RE MUCH TOO EASY TO PRAISE.

Without meaning to, parents can come across the same way. If we leave our praise unspoken, our criticism ends up being *de*structive, not *con*structive. Our goal may be to inject a bit of reality into our kids' dreams, but if we're not careful we can end up making a very different impact, inadvertently crushing them. And as the saying goes, with friends (or parents) like that, who needs enemies?

Top Tip: *Always ensure your **praise** heavily outweighs your **criticism**.*

The Management Technique of Nagging and Yelling

The irony of all this is that praise is extremely productive. A friend of mine talks about the management technique of 'nagging and yelling'. No one with any sense would run a business the way some people run their families, he says. If they did, pretty soon they wouldn't have a business left to run. And it's true. More and more business leaders are coming to realise that praise is profitable.

When you yell at people or nag them to get things done, all you do is gradually eat away at their enthusiasm for their job. Eventually they'll come to resent it, and you, so much that you'll get nothing more than the bare minimum out of them. But if you learn to praise people when they do well, they start to feel good about themselves and want to achieve more. Their confidence grows, and they do an even better job.

Praise will help your child recognise and then build on what they *can* do, working hard to overcome their weaknesses. By contrast, criticism will only make them feel bad about what they *can't* do, encouraging them simply to give up. So if you want to help your teenager make the right decision about what to do with their life, the most effective way to do it is to highlight the positive things about them, praising and encouraging them for the things they've done well.

Top Tip: *Praise is the miracle tool that'll help your teenager to bloom.*

Any Dream Will Do?

But does this mean that we should simply encourage our teenagers to do what they like with their lives? Is it responsible to let them shoot for the moon when we know they're afraid of heights? Or settle for mediocrity when we know they're capable of brilliance?

Well, yes and no. Of course we want the best for our children, and there are important things we can and should do to guide and support them as they make their decisions. But at the same time, we have to realise that the decisions *must* finally be theirs. As the saying goes, 'You can lead a horse to water, but you can't make it drink.' If, after all the discussion, your teenager still wants to be the world's first tone-deaf opera diva, you've got to let them make that decision. And however convinced you are that it's a mistake, they have to know that you're supportive of them. Sometimes we all have to make our own mistakes – but as they say, 'Wisdom is what you get when you don't get what you were expecting.'

On the other hand, there *are* things you can do to help them think again. But getting your approach right is key, because whether your teenager accepts or rejects your advice will, to a large extent, depend on how you go about presenting it. If you just set out to *tell* them what's wrong with their ideas, as far as they're concerned it'll seem like an unprovoked attack. As a result, they're bound to react in one of two ways. Either they'll take it personally and reject what you have to say altogether, assuming you're trying to decide their future *for* them; or they'll submit, with their confidence in their own ideas significantly eroded. In fact, they may even stop telling you about their ideas altogether – which means you'll lose all input into their decision-making process. Or perhaps worse still, they may begin watering down their dreams to such an extent that they'll never realise their full potential. None of this, of course, is what you want.

So rather than making patronising or dogmatic pronouncements on what your teenager should be thinking or doing, engage them in conversation and present your advice in the form of relaxed questions and suggestions, listening carefully and supportively to their views and answers. For instance, instead of *telling* your tone-deaf son that he hasn't got a hope in hell of ever joining the Three Tenors, *ask* him if he's thought about how he'll overcome his problem of not singing the right notes in quite the right order! Perhaps he thinks he has other, more developed, gifts and abilities?

Remember: your job is to help your teenager make their *own* decisions *good* decisions, not to make their decisions for them. So it's just as important to point out what's right with their thinking as it is gently to suggest areas where they may need to think again. If they know you're on their side, that you respect their independence, and that you'll support whatever decision they finally make (even if it's not the one you would have made), they'll be more open to your advice and suggestions in the future. If you're right and things don't quite go according to plan, they're more likely to feel able to come back and talk things through with you again – whereas if you tried to override and dismiss their views, you'll be the last person they'll turn to for help.

One last thought: remember all those times *you* rejected perfectly good advice, only to change your mind and accept it after you'd had a chance to think about it. Don't expect more from your teenager than you managed yourself.

Top Tip: *Don't patronise your teenager by presenting your advice to them as the only possible way forward.*

Decisions, Decisions ...

From the time they reach Year 10 and have to decide which GCSEs to do, your child will need to make a series of continuous choices about their future. How many GCSEs should they attempt? What options should they take? Should they go on to do A levels? Is it best to stay at school or take them at college? What kind of job are they best suited to? What about university? If so where, to do what? Should they take a gap year?

Helping your teenager to make career choices isn't a one-off, 'over and done' type of conversation. It's an ongoing issue that you need to chat through over time in as relaxed and informal a way as possible. Sitting your teenager down for a single, sombre, serious discussion about 'their future' in the lounge or their bedroom is almost guaranteed to put them off. And even if they make all the right noises, like the young Richard Branson, the exercise may not prove to be a very productive one in the long run.

Instead, try to create situations in which the subject can 'bubble to the surface' as naturally and casually as possible. The last thing you want is for your child to feel threatened or cornered by your questions, so choose your moments carefully. Obviously, the more time you naturally spend with them, the easier this will be. Make sure you've thought through what you're going to say, and that you're really going to listen to what *they* have to say. Do all you can to support and encourage them, as well as trying to ensure that they've thought seriously about their options and the real issues and obstacles they'll face. Help them constantly reassess their decisions, and take time to find out how they think they're getting on. Get them to think about 'contingency' options in case they don't hit all their goals, but never give them the impression you think their preferred choice is a non-starter.

 Top Tip: *Discuss your teenager's options in an ongoing way with them.*

The Big Picture

Part of helping your kids to make good career choices is letting them see the big picture. Your child is under enormous pressure to succeed, both at school and in society. As a result, like a hamster on a treadmill, they can become so focused on the future others have set before them – GCSEs, A levels, degree, good job, nice house, big salary, etc. – that they lose sight of what life's really all about.

My friend Tony is a university professor. He studied hard to get where he is and loves his job. But his best friend Bill had other ideas. He quit his job as a professor at the same university and became ... a postman! As far as Tony was concerned, this was more than just a waste of a good education. Bill was squandering his talents. But however hard he tried, Tony couldn't get him to 'see reason'. When he realised he'd never succeed, he changed tack. 'Well,' he told Bill, 'I hope at least that you're the best postman you could possibly be.'

'Actually,' Bill replied, 'I'm terrible! I start at the crack of dawn, but some days I just spend so long talking to people on their doorsteps that I don't finish my round until quite late in the day. But I wouldn't give it up for anything!' And actually, neither would the people who live on his round, who appreciate Bill so much they throw him a birthday party every year. To most of them he's a good and trusted friend. To some, especially the elderly or lonely, he's far more: he's a lifeline – the best friend they've got.

As a parent, it's your job to help your kids see that there's a lot more to school than good grades, and a lot more to life than a well-paid or 'respectable' job. There are lots of ways to measure 'success' and 'fulfilment', and most have nothing to do with the size of a person's salary. So as your teenager begins to make the kind of choices that will determine their career, help them to see how their schoolwork and preferred job fit into the context of their life as a whole.

 Top Tip: *Help your teenager to see that there's much more to life than fame and fortune.*

REMEMBER THERE'S MORE TO LIFE THAN FAME AND FORTUNE...
I KNOW, MUM - THERE'S CHOCOLATE TOO!

'It's All Gone Pear-shaped!'

<u>How Do I Help My Teenager Cope with Disappointment?</u>

In Disney's film *Toy Story*, Buzz Lightyear has a tough time coping with reality. It's a big come-down from thinking of himself as a Space Ranger on a mission from Star Command to 'protect the galaxy from the threat of invasion' to suddenly realising that he's nothing more than a kid's toy. Instead of coming to earth from somewhere up in the 'Gamma Quadrant', he discovers he was made in Taiwan. What difference does it make whether he lives or dies if all he amounts to in life is a child's plaything?

Coping with disappointment is part of life. It's something we all have to do. And it never gets easier to deal with. We just get more practised at it. There'll never be a time when any of us get past the point of being open to disappointment. The reason is simple: the potential for disappointment surrounds us constantly, no matter how young or old we are, whether it's other people, our own performance or life itself that lets us down. So by teaching your teenager how to handle failure, let-down and disappointment, you can be sure that you're equipping them with a vital skill they'll need

to use frequently, no matter how successful they become, for as long as they live.

Top Tip: *Coping with disappointment is a skill we all need all of our lives.*

The Way It Is

Life is competitive. Like it or not, that's simply the way it is. From school tests to job interviews, we're surrounded by competition all of the time. There's absolutely nothing we can do to change it. And because life is competitive, there are always going to be both winners and losers. There's nothing we can do to change that, either. But because no parent wants their child to fail, we tend to react in one of two ways. Some of us try to shield our kids from any form of competition. Others deliberately groom them for success. The truth is, both of these approaches are extremely short-sighted.

A few years ago, my family and I lived in a London borough where the local council believed that competition was unhelpful and negative. Aware that there are losers as well as winners in any competition, they also knew that society had already dealt many of the people in the borough a losing hand. So they'd developed a policy designed to shield children from being branded 'losers' early on in life by actively discouraging any form of competition. My son's school decided to put a total ban on all competitive sports.

It was one Saturday morning when he was about eight that the misguided nature of this approach really hit me. We were walking together through the local park and happened to stumble across a football match. He was totally amazed to see boys his own age dressed in full kit and playing in teams on a real pitch, complete with a referee! He stood and watched for a while and then, with a confused look on his face, asked me where the TV cameras were. I laughed. I only realised later that he'd been serious, because the only real football matches he'd ever seen were *professional* ones on the TV. He had no idea that other schoolboys – or anyone else, for that matter – played real matches in real kit, just for fun!

Trying to protect children from competition is more than just short-sighted. It's stupid. What's more, it's ultimately doomed to failure. Sooner or later, every child has to deal with the real world. That's why part of every responsible parent's job is to help their child learn how to cope with competition, rather than pretending that the world isn't really like that.

> **Top Tip:** Life is competitive. Pretending it's not is a recipe for disaster.

High Noon

But if trying to protect your teenager from competition is short-sighted, so is desperately trying to groom them for success, in the hope that if they're good enough they'll never have to deal with defeat or disappointment.

The truth is that failure is just as inevitable as competition. Whoever you are, you can't win everything. Your child, like you, will spend their whole life meeting people who're faster, cleverer, richer, kinder, more attractive or more inventive than they are. And it won't matter how good a tennis player, footballer, artist, musician, writer, speaker, actor, entrepreneur, racing driver or accountant they are, there'll always be someone faster, better or younger waiting to take their place.

A constant theme of old Hollywood Westerns was the gunfighter – the 'fastest draw in town'. No matter how reluctant or peaceful he was, once he'd carved out a name for himself as being quick on the draw, he had to keep defending his title – and with it his life! Young men, convinced they were faster and better, forced him into gunfights in the streets, getting themselves killed in the process. But for the gunfighter, staying at the top of his profession was just as difficult a challenge as getting there in the first place, and sooner or later he was bound to lose his edge: permanently.

Don't set your child up with the same kind of problem!

What's more, in the famous words of John Donne, 'No man is an island.' There isn't much in life that we do entirely on our own. Most of life is about being part of a team, whether at home, school, work, or anywhere else. So even if your teenager has achieved 'perfection', they'll still be let down by someone around them who hasn't. Since a team, like a chain, is only as strong as its weakest link, you can guarantee that sooner or later your teenager is going to be disappointed as a result of *someone's* performance, even if it isn't their own! So it's vital that you teach your son or daughter how to cope with disappointment and failure now, rather than postponing the lesson until later.

Top Tip: *Disappointment is inevitable, so don't put off teaching your teenager how to cope with it.*

Great Expectations

Some parents worry that by preparing their child for disappointment, they run the risk of actually setting them up to fail. They're afraid that mentioning the possibility of failure will guarantee its appearance. After all, if you teach your child that it doesn't matter if they fail or succeed, what incentive are you giving them to succeed? If you don't keep the pressure up, won't it just encourage them not to make the effort, settling for mediocrity when they're capable of so much more?

65

Though there are some parents who consciously or otherwise try to make up for their own failures and unfulfilled dreams by pushing their children to succeed in their place, for the vast majority of us our only motive is what's best for our child. We want to see them happy and fulfilled, and we naturally want them to do well. So we push them to work hard. There's nothing wrong with this, of course. In fact, if we didn't push them at all, they'd begin to wonder if we *cared* how they turned out. A bit of pressure and challenge is good for them. But it's a delicate balance, because *too much* pressure is crippling. Rather than being constructive, it becomes very destructive.

In the film *Dead Poets Society*, Neil's dad constantly pushes him to get good grades and become a doctor: a good, stable, prestigious job. To make him focus on his studies, he bans Neil from taking part in all out-of-school activities. Neil has other ideas. He secretly auditions for a local production of *A Midsummer Night's Dream*. He's extemely talented, and when he lands one of the lead roles in the play, he knows from that moment on what he wants to do with his life: become an actor.

When his dad finds out, he's furious. Though he loves his son immensely, and only wants the best for him, he's convinced that this means his becoming a doctor. After he's qualified, Neil can do what he likes with his spare time. In the meantime, what he needs most is something to knock this silly passion for acting out of him and focus his mind on his studies once and for all. So he decides to take Neil out of his strict and regimented school and send him to an even stricter and *more* regimented one!

The problem is that, to Neil, it seems that his dad will only love him on the condition that he stops being himself. Why can't he just accept him for who he is? Finally, when Neil realises that his dad will never let him become an actor, he spirals into depression which ends with him tragically taking his own life with his father's gun. His reasoning is simple: if his dad can't love him as he is, with no strings attached, it means he can't really love him at all. And since Neil desperately needs his dad's love and approval in order to cope with life, he can't see a way forward.

Top Tip: *Your teenager needs **some** pressure to perform at their peak, but **too much** can be crushing.*

'I Can't Get No Satisfaction!'

If your teenager suspects that you love them more when they succeed than when they fail, they'll naturally try to succeed in order to win your approval. But though this may seem to improve their grades or performance in the short term, it'll actually undermine their performance in the end. They'll slowly but surely stop believing that you love them unconditionally, and instead start to link your love with their achievement. When that happens, in pushing your child to succeed, you'll have ended up failing them.

What's more, whatever level of success they reach later in life, it'll never be enough to satisfy them. They'll always think you expect more, so they'll never be able to relax and enjoy the ride. Rather than being in control of their lives and able to enjoy the fruits of their labour, they'll be constantly driven by the need to try to live up to 'your' expectations.

My friend Peter is at the very top of his profession: wealthy, successful, charming and generous. But he's also unhappy. For over twenty years, he's been driven by the need to impress his dad, convinced he doesn't measure up to his expectations. Unfortunately, Peter's dad is dead. If he were still alive, I'm sure he'd be the proudest man on earth. But by giving Peter the impression, as a boy, that his love was conditional on achievement and success, he's condemned him to a life of empty ambition.

So try to maintain a healthy balance. On the one hand, try to ensure your child has high expectations of what they can achieve, challenging and equipping them to fulfill their true potential. On the other hand, don't crush them beneath unrealistic expectations that will not only put a straitjacket over their personality, but just as certainly fail to prepare them for the inevitable times of disappointment and frustration that lie ahead.

Of course, no one's pretending that failure doesn't matter. It does matter. Sometimes it matters a lot. It's just that you should try never to leave them with the impression that you love them any the less because they've failed at something.

Top Tip: *Never let your teenager think you love them more when they succeed than when they fail.*

'There, There, Dear ...'

So how *do* you help your teenager cope with disappointment when it comes their way? Well, to begin with, *don't* pretend that everything's OK when it's not. Even if it makes the immediate situation easier to deal with – and it can often make things worse – it won't help much in the long run.

If everything really *is* all right, and their sense of disappointment and failure is based on a faulty diagnosis of the situation, then telling them that it's all right and helping them see things more clearly will obviously help a lot. But if things *aren't* all right, pretending they are will just store up more trouble for both you and your child later on.

For one thing, you'll be denying them the chance to feel bad about what's happened, and that's a very necessary part of coping with disappointment. When someone experiences failure or disappointment, they very often go through a series of emotions similar to bereavement:

SHOCK ⇨ DENIAL ⇨ PAIN ⇨ ACCEPTANCE

By trying to short-cut these emotions, even with the best intentions in the world, you're essentially depriving your child of their opportunity to grieve. What's worse, you could even end up making them feel *bad* about feeling *bad*, further compounding the problem!

But most importantly, by telling your teenager that things are OK when they're not, you risk eroding the essential basis of your relationship with them: trust. They're likely to find out that you're being less than honest sooner or later, and that discovery will inevitably chip away at their trust in you. Even if your motives were as pure as the driven snow, they'll never again be completely sure that you're telling them the truth. So though you shouldn't necessarily volunteer the *whole* truth (if you know it's going to be painful to hear), be careful that you never deliberately deceive your teenager.

If they've failed or done worse than they'd hoped in their GCSEs, for example, there's nothing to be gained by saying they performed brilliantly. They'll know it's not true – they'll even have written proof of it right there in front of them! They'll be more likely to feel patronised than comforted, and that'll undermine their belief in you and your judgment. It would be far better to acknowledge their disappointment, but slowly help them see that the future isn't all bleak – even though it may only seem to consist of resits!

Top Tip: *Don't pretend your teenager's failure isn't real. Instead, show them it isn't the end.*

Being There

It's hard to watch the child you love feeling pain, but being there with them is the most important thing you can do. In fact, just 'being there' is probably the greatest help you can ever give someone who's trying to come to terms with failure, disappointment or loss. Don't feel you have to dole out advice, or keep talking to fill every silence. If your teenager doesn't want to talk, don't force them to. If they want to be alone, make a discreet exit. If they want to cry, offer them your shoulder to cry on. If they ask for advice or your opinion, give it to them truthfully. But never lose sight of the fact that you're helping them most just by being there for them. Your presence tells them that you love them, and you're there to give them whatever support they need.

When the famous classical composer Robert Schumann died, his friend Johannes Brahms, another brilliant composer, visited Schumann's widow. But on arriving at the house, he went straight to the piano, sat down, played some music and left – without uttering a single word. It was the best way he knew to honour his friend and tell Mrs Schumann how he felt about her husband's death. He couldn't find any words to express his grief, but, of course, no words were needed. The point was powerfully made without them. His presence was worth a thousand words to her.

Your teenager stopped expecting you to have all the answers a long time ago. They know you don't have a magic wand that can make everything better instantly. And even though you may have had 'exactly' the same experience they're going through when you were a teenager, they don't necessarily want to hear about it – even if they believe you! But they're never too old to be re-minded that you love them, and being there for them during the knocks and disappointments is a wonderful way of gently reassuring them how much you care. You don't have to say much, and they may not want to talk, but knowing that you still love them unconditionally is a way of helping them see that disappointment and failure aren't the end of the world. It helps to get things into perspective.

I have a friend whose son is a good runner. In fact, he's a *very* good runner. When he was chosen to compete for his school in a regional final, his parents couldn't have been more proud. Although he's not big for his age, he's fast. He trained hard to be in peak physical and mental condition. He could see himself crossing the finishing line, and he did – last. His opponents were the best in the region, and all of them were older, taller and quicker than he was.

He was devastated. When he got home afterwards, he ran straight up to his room and shut himself in, convinced he'd let himself and everyone else down. When his dad tried to talk to him, he looked more unhappy than ever. As they sat on his bed, he looked hard at the floor.

'Did you give it your best shot?' his dad asked.

'Yes,' he barked. He couldn't even blame the result on him having an 'off day'.

'Then I'm proud of you,' his dad said to him, getting up to leave. 'All I care about is that you give everything your best effort. It's great to win, but there's no shame at all in losing if you've given it your best shot.'

As his dad reached the door, the son said, 'You really do love me, don't you?'

We're always proud of our children when they do well, but doing well doesn't always mean coming first. It means applying yourself to the task, and using your abilities to their full potential: giving it your best shot. And as parents, we need to make sure that even when our kids don't win or succeed, they're still left in no doubt that we love them just as much anyway.

> **Top Tip:** *Being there for them tells your teenager that you love them, and that failure isn't the end of the road.*

'But the Good News is ...'

And that's why praise and encouragement are such important tools in building up your teenager's sense of self-worth. If *everything* you do seems to be wrong, then 'losing' can be a devastating blow. But when you know you're good at something else, failure is a lot easier to deal with. So by regularly praising your son or daughter for the things they do well, you'll help them to put their failures and weaknesses in context. By telling your teenager what's good about them, you'll enable them to develop the courage to face up to, and cope with, their limitations in other areas.

Some people's abiding memory of school is the humiliation of constantly being picked last when it came to sports teams. My eldest daughter is aware that she's hardly God's gift to sports. But this isn't something she finds too hard to come to terms with, because she also knows she's strong in other areas. For instance, she's the only sixteen-year-old I know who not only understands but *enjoys* reading Shakespeare. *I* used to hate it! Cornelia and I have tried hard to encourage her in the things she likes and the things she's good at. And as a result of knowing her strengths, I hope she's learning more easily to accept her weaknesses.

Archie Graham, one of the heroes in the film *Field of Dreams*, quits professional baseball after just one season. Having dreamt of becoming a famous batsman all season, he's frustrated by the coach's refusal to let him prove what he can do. He's never given the chance to hit a single ball in a game, and he only gets to field once. So he decides to quit and study medicine instead. When he's an old man, a young friend asks him if he's ever regretted his decision: 'Fifty years ago, for five minutes, you came *this* close. It would kill some men to get that close and not touch it. They'd consider it a tragedy.'

But Archie's had a whole lifetime to think about the decision he made, and he has no regrets. He knows he's a good doctor, and he's made a real diffence in people's lives. Without being at all arrogant, he's rightly proud of what he's achieved in life. This is what gives him the strength to cope with the disappointment of having come so close to his dreams, but not having been given the chance to achieve them.

'Son,' he replies, 'if I'd only gotten to be a doctor for five minutes, now that would have been a tragedy.'

Top Tip: *Re-emphasising your teenager's strengths will help them cope with their weaknesses.*

Snatching Victory from the Jaws of Defeat

The truth is, of course, that failure and disappointment can be much better teachers than success. We often learn more about ourselves – including our strengths and weaknesses – when we fail at something than when we succeed.

When Helen failed her university degree, she was gutted. Neither she nor her teachers could believe it. They all knew she was clever, but everything had been riding on her project. At first she wondered if they'd marked the wrong one by mistake! But then, as she started going over it again in her mind with a fine tooth comb, she began to see *why* they'd failed her. Ignoring her weaknesses, she'd made the mistake of overestimating her strengths and over-stepped the limits of her expertise. In other words, the examiners hadn't failed her for not being good enough. They'd failed her for not being disciplined enough to *stick* to the areas where she was good enough.

It was a painful lesson, but failing gave Helen a far better insight into her strengths and weaknesses than she'd ever had before. It brought her face to face with her own limitations, but it also helped her to see far more clearly where her skills and talents lay. And it's this vital knowledge that's helped her to cope with her disappointment. She'll know better next time, when there may be more at stake than just a university degree.

In the same way, if you can help your child face and cope with their disappointments, they'll have a chance to put them in perspective, learn from them and move on as a stronger and wiser person.

 Top Tip: *Failure can teach your teenager their limits, but you can also use it to teach them their strengths.*

A Matter of Opinion

How Do I Help My Teenager Cope with Conflicting Views and Influences?

In 1740, the HMS *Centurion* set sail for the South Pacific. As it rounded Cape Horn, at the very tip of South America, a fierce storm blew it days off course. The ship's supplies of fresh fruit and vegetables ran out, and illness slowly began to claim the lives of the ship's crew. When the storm was finally over, the captain sailed west as quickly as he could for the nearest British colony, Juan Fernandez Island, for the fresh supplies they so deperately needed.

Back then, however, it was impossible for sailing ships to pinpoint with any accuracy just where they were. So after several days with no sight of land, the captain began to panic. He knew he was on the right line, but he had no way of telling how much further west he needed to travel, or even if the storm had carried him beyond Juan Fernandez in the first place. Deciding they had to be heading in the wrong direction, he turned the ship around to sail east.

But a few days later, disaster struck. They reached Spanish-held Chile, and he realised he'd been right the first time. They must have been only a few hours away from Juan Fernandez when he'd ordered the about turn. They couldn't get supplies from Chile: it was enemy territory. So they were forced to turn around again and head back the way they'd come. By the time they eventually reached Juan Fernandez, more than half of the five hundred crew members were dead. If only the captain had stuck to his convictions and trusted his initial judgment, many lives would have been spared. But making up your mind about things in the thick of the action is never easy.

Of course, thanks to chronometers, satellite tracking and air-sea rescue, your teenager will never have to go through that kind of experience, even if they become a sailor. But whatever course they choose in life, they'll certainly have their convictions tested. They might not be sent physically zigzagging across the Pacific Ocean like the HMS *Centurion*, but at times they're bound to feel as if they're being pushed from pillar to post when it comes to trying to understand the world they live in and forming their own opinions and moral code.

Your teenager lives in a world where they're constantly bombarded by different views on sex, drugs, music, politics, the environment, money, fashion, religion, war, animal rights, homosexuality, careers, food, art, transport, race, gender, language, sport – the list is endless. Some of these opinions are just other people's opinions. But many are deliberate attempts to persuade them that a particular view is the one they *should* have. Rightly or wrongly, there's a real battle going on for your teenager's mind (and money)!

 Top Tip: *Your teenager needs your help learning to navigate through life.*

A Chip off the Old Blockhead?

In the first few years of their life, your child actively *wanted* to copy everything you did and said. You were their hero, and they wanted to be exactly like you. Nothing mattered more to them than what you thought. But now, as they reach the teenager years, that time is past. They're beginning to explore the freedom to make their own decisions and form their own opinions. At the same time, you're having to learn what this new-found freedom means as what they do and say becomes increasingly beyond your control.

But the truth is that you're *still* a vital role model for your teenager, even though they now have many other influences on their life. Not only did what they learnt from you *as a child* play a vital part in forming the foundations on which they're now building their own distinct personality and approach to life, but they're actually *still* learning from you in much the same way. If you're honest and kind, for example, they're more likely to be honest and kind. If you're rude or arrogant, they're more likely to be rude or arrogant. If you're unfaithful, they're more likely to be promiscuous. If you're lazy, they may end up the same. And if you use violence and bullying to get your way, don't blame them if they catch the habit.

We've all heard about identical twins, separated at birth, who've got the same taste in food, clothes, music – even the opposite sex. Our genes play a key role in determining the kind of person we turn out to be. But our character is also undoubtedly shaped by our influences, our choices and our upbringing. So we've also heard about identical twins, separated at birth, who turn out completely

different. In other words, 'nature' and 'nurture' *both* play a part in deciding who we are and what we're like as people.

You can't do anything about your teenager's genes. He or she got them from you and is stuck with them (which is a good reason for being tolerant of their shortcomings). But you *can* do lots to influence their personality, and help them make sense of the mass of conflicting advice and opinions they're being exposed to all the time.

Every parent has the huge responsibility and the wonderful privilege of being a role model, moulding someone who will one day perhaps become a parent themselves. Beyond doubt, the way we parent our children is the single biggest factor in determining how they turn out. One day, they'll look in the mirror and realise just how much like us they've become. We're all role models, influencing our child's opinions and morality. The only question is, what kind of role models are we?

Top Tip: *You're a role model to your teenager – so watch out!*

Under the Influence

Some parents are very worried about imposing their morals on their kids. They're afraid of over-influencing them, or even brainwashing them. But the truth is, even if *you're* not interested in shaping your teenager's values, everyone else *is*. Your child is being bombarded by a huge array of influences all of the time. Even the idea that they could be given a 'value-free' education at school is now dead and buried. Teachers realise that something of their own values always creeps in, no matter how objective they try to be.

A few years ago, I went to South Africa to make a TV programme. One of the people I interviewed for it was the famous Nobel Peace Prize winner, Dr Bayers Naudé. Although he'd been a fierce opponent of apartheid for more than twenty-five years, Dr Naudé told me that as a young man training to be a priest, he'd honestly believed that apartheid was 'God's will for South Africa'. It's what he'd been taught as a boy. It's what his friends and colleagues believed. And even though he was a very clever man, he'd never thought to question it. 'Apartheid was simply taken for granted,' he said.

Teenagers are like sponges, soaking up their values from the world around them. So the question isn't, 'Is your child being brainwashed?' It's 'What are your child's brains being washed with?' If you're not influencing them, you're about the only person in their life who isn't. Everyone else is doing it for you, but with *their* values and standards rather than *yours*.

The experts tell us that the average dad spends just three minutes a day in 'quality' conversation with their kids. The average mum does slightly better, knocking up five and a half minutes. By contrast, the average child spends three hours a day watching TV. In fact, some teenagers have TVs in their bedrooms, and many sitting rooms are arranged around the TV just like a mini-cinema. The only things some families seem to do together are eat and watch television, and even eating takes the form of 'grazing' in front of the Box.

So it doesn't take Einstein to work out that TV is a major influence in your teenager's life. It helps shape their values, morals and beliefs. But they're also constantly being influenced by school, music, magazines, computers, radio, advertising, books, videos, other adults, pressure groups, friends and even friends' parents. In fact, they're exposed to an overwhelming barrage of views and values every day of their lives.

This kind of exposure is bewildering enough for adults. We often find it hard to know who to believe when people or papers give us quite different versions of events. From who hit whom first in the home, to who did what in the office, or which political party is telling us the truth about some issue or another (if any of them ever do), it can be tough to know whom to trust. But for teenagers, who've only just stopped believing everything everyone tells them, it's even more difficult. But *you* can help.

Top Tip: You can't stop your teenager being brainwashed, but you can at least choose the washing powder!

Whatever You Want

Of course, you can and should limit the influences your teenager is exposed to. I heard a self-appointed 'agony uncle' explain on a radio chat show a few months ago how, in his opinion, teenagers are adults and should therefore be allowed to do whatever they like. But, in fact, he couldn't be more wrong. Teenagers *aren't* adults. They're adolescents – 'in-betweeners'. Legally, they're not adults until they're eighteen, and there's a reason for this: they've still got a lot to learn. So just as no one in their right mind would let an L-plated driver loose on a crowded motorway, a wise parent tries to protect their teenager from the most destructive influences around, whilst at the same time preparing and equipping them to handle those influences when they're older.

It's a vital part of every parent's responsibility to monitor what their child sees on TV or video or at the cinema, what they read in books and magazines, and where they go with their friends, etc. It's part of the framework of guidelines and boundaries that a loving parent sets for their child to teach them to handle freedom within safe limits. It won't always make you popular, of course, and your teenager may not believe you when you tell them *why* they're not allowed to watch a particular programme or go and see a particular film, especially if you use the phrase, 'It's for your own good' (which it *is*!). But the boundaries still have to be there.

Some people argue that it's a waste of time forbidding your teenager to do something, as they'll only go and do it anyway somewhere else, behind your back. Forbidding your teenager may not always be the best course of action – there are often other ways of tackling the issues – but that doesn't take away from the fact that rules and limits *are* important, even when they get broken. They send a message about what kind of behaviour is acceptable and, more to the point, safe. Take the speed limit, for example. Most of us have broken this at one time or another, whether deliberately or not. No one suggests that it's universally effective. But just think of the chaos that would arise if our narrow roads had no speed restrictions whatsoever. Some kind of limit has to be there, and be enforced with penalties, in spite of the fact that it will still get broken.

Top Tip: *If you don't set limits, your teenager won't know when to stop.*

Vacuum-packed?

But here's the twist: trying too hard to protect your teenager is a big mistake. The more you create a hermetically sealed environment for them, the less you actually prepare them for the real world they'll encounter when they finally leave home. And you can't keep them locked up for ever, even if you wanted to.

As a young boy, I was fed on a diet of cartoons, films and fairy stories, which *always* had a happy ending. From the daring adventures of Robin Hood, triumphing over injustice and the evil Sheriff of Nottingham, to Scrooge in Dickens' famous novel, *A Christmas Carol*, learning that there's more to be gained from

85

generosity than greed – good always won out!

But real life is different. Good *doesn't* always win. Life *isn't* always fair. It can be a bitch. And if *we* don't prepare our teenagers for reality, who will? If we cocoon them away from all harm and danger, they'll only be safe as long as we maintain the cocoon. As a result, they'll be at a massive disadvantage when they leave home, or if anything unexpected happens and we can't protect them any longer. So preparation is the key.

We all know water can be dangerous, and every parent keeps a watchful eye out when they take their young children anywhere near a lake, river or swimming pool because they could so easily fall in. But what's the best way of preparing them for this unfortunate possibility – to keep them permanently away from water, or to teach them to swim? The wise choice, made by millions, is, of course, swimming lessons. No surprises there. So why should we consider anything other than preparation when it comes to helping our kids deal with the mess of conflicting influences, views or opinions they're exposed to every day? The risk of 'riskless living' is the greatest risk of all.

 Top Tip: *You can't protect your teenager from the harshness of life, but you* **can** *prepare them for it!*

The Other Side of the Coin

So your *real* job isn't to closet your teenager away, but to help them understand and cope with conflicting influences and opinions better. And the best way of doing that is to talk to them about the issues they face or see on TV, rather than ignoring them or sweeping them under the carpet.

A couple of years ago, my friend Claire was so concerned about the values being peddled by a particular TV soap that she banned her teenagers from watching it. But the plan backfired. They ended up feeling like outcasts, since all their friends had seen the show the night before and were talking about it at school. What's more, they weren't even being 'protected' from the values that had made Claire so worried about the show. They were just hearing them second-hand, sometimes considerably ampified for effect!

When she finally realised this, Claire changed tactics. She decided to let them watch it and watch it with them herself. That way, they could chat about the show's contents afterwards. And without being overbearing or forceful, but presenting the other side of the coin, she could get her kids to think about what they'd seen, weighing up the values and opinions the show presented to see if they made sense in the long run.

Sometimes helping your teenager cope with conflicting views means nothing more than that: showing them the other side of the coin. You can help them to think through their own ideas by exposing them to the opposing views and opinions. But don't be confrontational. Be gentle. Be careful not to tear into them or their views. If you do, they'll just defend their position all the harder, whether it's true or not. We often reject advice, not because it's no good, but simply because it's given in such a way that we feel got at. The instinctive response to any attack is to batten down the hatches and become more entrenched than ever. The next response is to hit back. The one thing we *don't* do is listen.

 Top Tip: *Help your teenager think through their ideas by gently putting forward an alternative view.*

Pass the Parcel

Passing on your values won't happen overnight. Unfortunately, you can't just sit your teenager down for 'The Mammoth, Six-Hour, Big-Value Talk' and hope that'll do the trick. Teenagers are notorious for appearing to ignore or disbelieve almost everything their mum or dad tells them. The reason is simple: whilst they still value and want to hear your opinions, they've also got to develop and safeguard their new independence. They've got to have time to mull things over a bit, slowly deciding whether or not to turn *your* opinions into *their own* values. So don't expect them automatically to accept your opinions and moral views as gospel truth.

What's more, this isn't a process you can rush. It takes a long time, like filling a bath from a dripping tap.

So start NOW! And remember, values are both *caught* and *taught*.

• **Values are caught.** Many of your values are passed on *accidentally*. From long before they were able to make 'value judgments', your child will have been copying what you say and do. Both consciously and unconsciously, they'll have adopted your gestures and mannerisms as well as some of your values. So if you don't want your child to learn something from you, don't do it. The old adage, 'Do as I say, not as I do', never works. Whatever you tell your teenager about your values, they'll check to see how it all works out in practice in your life. If you try to teach them values you don't actually live by, they'll know it. And they'll come to the obvious conclusion: you're a hypocrite. Then they'll probably reject your values, and maybe even you as well. So get your act up to scratch. If you want them to do it, make sure they see you doing it. If you don't want them to do it, make sure you don't do it either. If you're not convinced that your values are worth passing on, then change them *now*! Because if they're not worth passing on, they're not worth having.

- **Values are taught.** But of course, it's not enough to hope your teenager will catch your values just because they see them. If they don't understand them properly, they won't be of any use to them. So work hard to find opportunities when you can deliberately pass on your advice, wisdom, views, opinions and beliefs to them. It would be tragic if, when they left home, your child didn't know what you felt about life's most important issues. So make sure they know *why* you hold the values you do. Sit down with them for a quiet one-on-one chat over breakfast, or dinner in a restaurant. (It needn't be expensive: you're there for the conversation, not the food.) Take them to the cinema and talk about the issues the film raises. Or talk to them while you're both doing something together. Whatever you do, don't put it off. Start this week, or the next time you turn around, it'll be too late.

Your teenager is just leaving harbour and setting sail on life's voyage, and they're not always that good at handling the rudder yet. They haven't had the chance to learn how to make consistently mature and sensible decisions, or how to filter all the opinions that bombard them. So it's your job to help them steer. It's your responsibility as their mum or dad to stand beside them at the helm, guiding and advising them as they turn the rudder. This isn't just a duty, it's also a wonderful and extremely exciting privilege. So don't miss out on it.

 Top Tip: *Your values need to be both **caught** and **taught**.*

PART THREE: FRIENDS

'Does My Bum Look Big in This?'

How Can I Help My Teenager Develop a Positive Self-Image?

I like *Star Trek*. To be perfectly honest, I'm a bit of a 'Trekkie'. It may be sad, but it's the way I am. In one riveting episode of *Star Trek: The Next Generation*, Federation scientist Bruce Maddox plans to disassemble Commander Data. Data is an android: a machine built to walk, talk and think just like a human being. But since Data's creator is now dead, Maddox wants to take him to bits in order to understand how he works. The idea is that if they know how he works, they can then make more androids like him. Maddox promises he has the ability to put Data back together again properly afterwards. But Data isn't convinced. He refuses to be disassembled because, he says, there's nothing like him in the universe – if Maddox can't reassemble him properly, something unique will be lost.

Data is right. But what's true of an android is doubly true of your teenager. Without them becoming big-headed or arrogant, you want them to know that the world is a better place for having them in it. You want them to realise how unique and valuable they are. There's no one else quite like them, with their particular mix of tastes and talents, and that makes them very special.

I'M GLAD YOU THINK I'M SPECIAL, MUM... BUT LET'S KEEP THE FACT THAT I CAN BURP "BOHEMIAN RHAPSODY" TO YOURSELF

Top Tip: *Let your teenager know they're special just because they're them.*

Happy Ever After?

A few years ago, a friend of mine gave me some good advice.

'Almost everyone you'll meet in life is struggling to cope with one thing or another,' he said. 'They're carrying around some kind of emotional burden. So try not to add to their troubles. Instead, do what you can to lighten their load a little bit.' Over the years, I've come to see how true that advice was.

A friend recently told me the tragic story of a fifteen-year-old girl called Sarah. She'd always been a little on the heavy side, even as a baby. Her mum and dad never praised or complimented her, and she couldn't remember them ever telling her they loved her. At school, she faced constant taunts and put-downs because of her weight. Sarah didn't like herself, convinced she was ugly and unloved.

Then, one day, her class had to play a game where they imagined they were survivors of a terrible shipwreck. They'd made it to the lifeboat, but there wasn't enough room for everyone. After a heated discussion, they came up with reasons why they *all* had to be on board if they were ever going to make it to dry land. All, that is, except Sarah. 'Besides,' one boy joked, 'she *is* the heaviest.' That night Sarah committed suicide. In a note telling her story, she said she'd always hoped to marry a handsome prince one day and live happily ever after. She couldn't bear living now she knew he'd never come.

We all go through times in our lives when we wonder if other people like us. We're not sure we've got anything special to give. But teenagers feel this acutely. However loud or confident your teenager sounds, they need your constant reassurance that you love them and that they're very special. Just like Commander Data, something uniquely valuable would be lost if anything were to happen to them.

Top Tip: *Your teenager needs constant reassurance that they're special.*

Strength for the Journey

Throughout life, your teenager, like you, will find themselves being accepted or rejected on the basis of how they perform. It's the way of the world, and a hard lesson to learn. But like it or not, they'll slowly discover that most people are interested in them, not because of who they are, but simply because of their looks, their skills, their contacts or their money – in short, because they have something others want.

As a mum or dad, it's *your* job to be the exception to this rule. You've got to show your child that you love and accept them, not for what they can achieve, but for who they are – with no strings attached. They need to know they can trust you when you say you love them.

We all need this kind of unconditional, 'no strings attached' love to be truly happy. If we never receive it, we end up heading through life trying to please people in order to *make* them like or love us, crippled by our fear that we'll accidentally do something to make them *stop* liking or loving us. What's more, if we've never known unconditional love, there's a danger that we'll get our three basic human needs – love, security and significance – confused with sex, money and power. The consequences are always disastrous.

At the extreme end, not being sure that you're loved unconditionally can lead to tragic illnesses like anorexia nervosa or bulimia nervosa. What's more, according to the Joseph Rowntree Foundation, children who feel rejected by their parents are more likely to be sexually promiscuous as teenagers than those whose homes are secure. In other words, if your child isn't sure you love them unconditionally, they'll most likely go looking for love elsewhere. And very often, they'll end up looking in all the wrong places.

If life is a journey, *unconditional* love – loving your child for who they are, not what they do – is about giving them the strength and inner resources to enjoy the journey. By showing your child you love them unconditionally, you're proving to them that they're an intrinsically valuable and individually unique human being, regardless of what they can do or what assets they have.

 Top Tip: *Unconditional love is the fuel we **all** need for life's journey.*

Act Naturally

Of course, loving their kids unconditionally isn't hard for most parents. In fact, it comes naturally. I don't think I really knew how I'd feel about being a dad until I held my first child in my arms. But from the moment I did, I knew I'd *always* love her, no matter what she did or failed to do in her life. I didn't love her because of what she could offer or do for me, or because of her personality. I loved her because I loved her, and for no other reason. That's unconditional love.

There's an instant, natural, biological bond of love between mums and their kids. And even for dads, who haven't carried the child for nine months, there's a kind of irresistible magnetism. A baby's big eyes, little face, gawky behaviour and vulnerability all draw out our parental instincts. In fact, some scientists say that babies deliberately evolved to look like this in order to trigger our parental and loving instincts, and to get us oohing and aahing.

The feeling isn't entirely one-sided, of course. Children grow up instinctively loving and trusting their parents. They want and need our attention and acceptance. But whilst toddlers take it for granted that we love them, teenagers have reached the age where they're questioning all their previous assumptions – including our unconditional love for them. So we need to work hard to give them absolute proof positive we still love them, and we'll always love them, no matter what they do. That way, we'll have given them the right foundations not only to survive life, but to thrive on it.

Foundations are vital. Without them, you're in big trouble. In 1994, six months after a devastating earthquake, I visited Maharashtra State in India. Though the blast hadn't measured very high on the Richter scale, more than 25,000 people had lost their lives in just forty seconds. The damage was almost unbelievable. In one village, every house was totally demolished except for one, which was completely untouched – it didn't even have a crack in the plaster. When I asked why, I was told that it belonged to a rich man. In a village built basically of stones, mud and wood, it was the only home made from bricks and mortar on a proper foundation. Had all the houses been built like this one, no one would have lost their life, or even been seriously injured.

Being a parent is a wonderful experience, but it's also a huge responsibility. What we do today lays the foundations for what our teenager becomes tomorrow. Andrew, a forty-year-old friend of mine, claims he's still basically a 'prisoner of his childhood'. And he's not alone. Some people spend years and a small fortune on therapy sessions, trying to sort out emotional problems related to the murky depths of their childhood. So give your teenager a solid bedrock to build on: let them know you love them unconditionally.

Top Tip: *Unconditional love is the foundation of a healthy, happy life.*

A Brief History of Time

So how do we let our teenager know we love them unconditionally, and that they're a unique and special individual? Well, the first and most important thing is – spend time with them. In the 1980s, it was fashionable to believe that it didn't really matter *how much* time you spent with your child so long as it was 'quality time'. People told themselves that if they set aside 'power time' with their kids – filled with intense, quality activity – they'd have adequately fulfilled their obligation as a mum or dad. But sadly, it doesn't work like that.

One of the clearest ways a teenager has of measuring the *quality* of time you spend with them is by looking at its sheer *quantity*. After all, when you love someone, you want to spend as much time with them as you can. So if they get the impression you don't want to spend time with them, it's logical for them to assume that you don't really love them, whatever else you might say. (Of course, it won't matter *how* much time you spend with them if, even in doing so, you give them the impression that you don't really want them around!)

When someone casually asks in a passing conversation, 'How are you?', what's your reply? 'OK, thanks.' It's the standard answer, even if the truth is actually very different. Very few of us wear our hearts on our sleeves. For most of us, it takes a huge amount of courage, and time, to open up and tell someone our innermost thoughts, feelings and problems. When we share our most private and personal thoughts with someone, we're letting them know what we're *really* like deep down inside, and that always carries with it the risk that they won't like us. It's a big gamble to take. If they *do* like us, we can be sure they like us for who we really are, and that's a big boost to our self-esteem. But if they *don't*, it can be crippling. So we only tend to share our most personal thoughts with people we trust, and trust isn't usually built quickly.

Your teenager needs to know that you love them for who they really are. And in spite of the fact that they once took this love for granted, it'll still take them time to trust you enough to realise that you've never stopped loving them for who they are, and never will. Important conversations don't happen on cue. The biggest issues or questions only trickle out because a parent is *there*. In fact, teenagers have a habit of asking the deepest questions at the oddest and most inappropriate times.

Quality-Time-Power-Chats are always an intimidating prospect, and rarely achieve more than giving you the chance to offload some of your own guilt or frustration. So try to make yourself available – only by investing *quantity* time will you reap the chance of a *quality* conversation. When you're making the tea, playing on the computer together, out swimming, bowling, or watching TV or a football match together, you'll find that your teenager may raise one of those all-important issues right 'out of the blue'.

Most of the best conversations I've had with my kids about careers, racism, bullying, love, failure, success, honesty, money, relationships, justice, etc., have started like this. Being around for your child sends them the message, 'I enjoy your company. I'm glad you're here.' And it reassures them that it's safe to talk openly without fear of rejection – which again underlines the fact that you love them unconditionally.

Top Tip: *Without **quantity** time, you'll never build a **quality** relationship with your teenager.*

'I've Pencilled You In for between the News and the Weather ...'

Making quantity time for your teenager is tough, and there's no secret formula for success, except to keep working hard at it day after day. It's like walking a tightrope. It's not a case of struggling initially to get your balance and then, having done so, finding that you're free to carry on regardless. Staying upright on the high wire is a *continuous* process of making tiny, but absolutely vital, adjustments.

I'M GOING TO WORK OUT HOW YOU AND I CAN SPEND QUALITY TIME TOGETHER AS SOON AS I GET A GAP IN MY SCHEDULE.

It's too easy to blame your job, or the housework, or both, for the lack of time you have to spend with your child. But in fact, contrary to popular opinion, the major tensions that arise from competing home and work pressures aren't really anything to do with the type of job or responsibilities you or your partner has. They're actually more to do with you and your *personality*.

It took me a long time to wake up to this. My workaholic tendencies have little or nothing to do with what I do for a living. Instead, they're part of *me*. I'd have been just as busy if I'd become a banker, plumber, salesman, journalist, gardener, milkman, doctor or lawyer. It's uncomfortable to admit it, but when we blame 'work' for our failure to give our family the time and support they need, we're kidding ourselves. I'm not trying to dismiss work pressures. I know all too well how real they are. It's just that going *out* to work doesn't excuse anyone from coming *home* to work.

Those of us who work outside the home can't just decide to turn off once we're inside the front door. However much we might want to, we can't just put our feet up in front of the TV and switch off. I can't excuse myself from involvement with my children and my share of the chores on the grounds that I've been 'working hard all day'. It's a fatal mistake for someone in paid employment to behave as though 'work' stops the moment they leave the site or finish sifting through papers. The truth is, we need to work every bit as hard at our home life as we do in our workplace. But don't despair: making an effort at home isn't just the right thing to do – it's also incredibly rewarding!

Of course, balancing family and work is never easy. But then, it's not easy finding the time to mix a passion for work with a passion for swimming, football, squash, bowling, fishing, golf or even the pub, club or gym – yet busy men and women have managed it for years. The very undramatic truth is that the decisions *can* be made – if we're prepared to make them. As they say, 'Where there's a will, there's a way'.

In the film *Beethoven* George and his wife Alice argue about the family dog, which is ruining his business plans. 'My dreams are going down the drain and you're worried about a dog?' he yells. 'Your family is going down the drain and you're worried about a dream!' she replies.

The truth is that, like it or not, how you're doing at work just *isn't* a big priority for your child. By the time they're a teenager, they're unimpressed by what you do. They don't care about your promotion, the size of your pay packet or your public profile. But they *do* care about you, and they need to know that you care about *them*. So make time for them while you still can, before the opportunities are gone for ever.

 Top Tip: *Make sure your teenager is a high priority in your life.*

The Power of Positive Thinking

Teenagers, like adults, feel good about themselves when they know they're doing well. And they know they're doing well when they're *told* they're doing well. Ivan Pavlov was awarded the Nobel Prize for Medicine in 1904 for his work on what we now call 'conditioned responses'. He found that if he rang a bell when he fed his dog, the dog associated the bell with food. After a while, whenever he rang the bell, the dog *expected* food. Like it or not, the truth is that *we* react in much the same way. We make choices, of course, but we also make mental 'associations' and act accordingly.

So when Luciano Pavarotti performed in London a few years ago, the audience surprised him by trying to sing along to one of the songs on the programme. But while Pavarotti sang 'O Sole Mio', the audience chanted 'Just One Cornetto'. TV adverts from years before had firmly linked the old tune with ice cream.

We all understand the power of a negative mental 'association'. That's why we punish our kids for doing something bad. We're relying on them associating their punishment with their 'crime'. We hope it'll make them think twice next time. But positive associations are just as important. Your teenager *needs* to feel valued and appreciated. So if you praise them when they do something right, they'll be more likely to do it again. And if you praise them for putting in the effort, they'll want to try just as hard, if not harder, in the future.

Just as a flower blossoms when you give it enough water, and dies when you neglect it, so your child's self-esteem will bloom when you praise them and wither when you don't. Experts call this the Law of Reinforcement – 'behaviour which achieves desirable consequences will recur' – but to most of us it's plain, old-fashioned common sense. Whether it's spoken or written down in a card or letter (so they can read it to themselves again and again in the privacy of their own room), praise will help your teenager's self-image to blossom.

 Top Tip: *Catch your teenager red-handed doing something right – and praise them for it!*

The Seven Steps to Happiness

As you praise your teenager, be careful to steer clear of the following common pitfalls:

103

1 **Avoid fake praise.** Never allow your desire to praise your child to push you into lying to them. Insincere praise never helps. Not only is it patronising, it'll devalue any genuine praise you offer them on other occasions.

2 **Avoid vague praise.** Always be specific. If your teenager knows *exactly* what they did right, they'll learn to recognise their strengths. Don't just say, 'That was good.' Explain *why* it was good.

3 **Avoid achievement-related praise.** If your teenager begins to link your approval and love with their success, the self-esteem you're trying to build will be destroyed. So praise them for their effort, choices, thoughtfulness, independence, skills, ideas or helpfulness, *not* just for success itself.

4 **Avoid qualified praise.** If you follow your praise with a lecture on how they could have done *even better* if only they'd done this or that, you'll send your teenager the message that their effort wasn't good enough. They'll remember the criticism, but not the praise. (Experts reckon it takes eighteen pieces of praise to counteract the effects of just *one* piece of negative criticism!)

5 **Avoid comparative praise.** Never say, 'You were better than so and so.' And above all, don't praise your teenager for being 'the best'. Doing *their* best is what counts. Help them to measure their effort against *their* standards, not someone else's.

6 **Avoid manipulative praise.** Never praise people to 'warm them up' for a favour – 'That's great, love … Now get us a cup of tea, will you?' Even if your praise is real, by linking it to a request you'll make it seem insincere.

7 **Avoid material praise.** Don't give incentives: 'If you do well in your GCSEs, I'll get you that new stereo system you wanted.' If they fail, you'll find yourself having to withhold a present at just the time your teenager needs to feel your love and acceptance the most. And the situation's not much better if they succeed. If you want to give your teenager a gift, give it, being careful not to spoil them. But never use treats as incentives.

Top Tip: *Praise helps your teenager identify their strengths, which helps them to see their unique value.*

Behind the Bike Sheds

How Do I Deal with My Teenager's Boyfriends/Girlfriends?

Sally slowly descends the staircase. Her delicate poise, blonde hair, perfect complexion and flawless make-up give her dramatic descent into the hall an almost regal appearance. But what catches her father's eye is the way her plunge-neckline, pencil-strap, spray-on white minidress accentuates her slim fifteen-year-old figure.

'What the hell do you think you're playing at, young lady?' he yells. 'You're not going out in *that*! It looks like underwear! It'll get you into no end of trouble. Go right upstairs this minute and take it off! No, I mean – stretch it! Put something decent on!'

Even the easiest-going parents tend to get uptight when it comes to their child and sex. Sexual decisions are the most intimate we can make. And sexual mistakes are often the most painful. In fact, it's no exaggeration to say that they can even be lethal. This means that teenage sexuality is as big a minefield for a parent as it is for their child. We want to trust our teenager to make their own decisions. But we also want them to make good decisions: ones that'll keep them safe from harm. It can be hard to adjust to the fact that the five-year-old we used to help dress is now a sexually aware fifteen-year-old who inhabits an increasingly private world filled with their own choices.

In the Middle Ages, some fathers resorted to locking up their daughters in chastity belts as a guaranteed method of ensuring their purity. And out of love, concern and even fear for our children, it's sometimes easy to wish we could do the same kind of thing today. But the truth is that it didn't work then and wouldn't work now. Even back in medieval days, enterprising manacled daughters ended up bedding the handsome young blacksmith's apprentice in order to get a spare key cut. Nowadays they'd simply buy a Junior Hacksaw, learn how to pick the lock, or report you to Social Services!

I have a friend who tells me that as soon as his daughter reaches her teenage years, he plans to keep a couple of large, hungry, ferocious Alsatian dogs to protect her from 'the wrong kind of boys'. 'If they try anything,' he says, 'the dogs will soon sort them out!' But sadly, this strategy is also doomed to failure. Sooner or later, his daughter will find a boyfriend with enough brains to buy some nice, juicy steaks to distract the dogs. Or, alternatively, she'll just go round to his place! And as a result, my friend will have even less influence and control over the situation than ever.

Instead, our goal must be to *educate* our teenagers about sex, informing them about their choices and the possible consequences of these choices. A wise parent makes it their goal to equip their teenager with a kind of internal 'chastity belt'. In other words, they do their best to instil in them the only things that can ultimately help and guide them: wisdom, self-esteem and self-control.

DAD, WHY DO YOU LIKE THAT STORY ABOUT THE PRINCESS LOCKED IN A TOWER?

IT GIVES ME IDEAS OF HOW TO COPE WHEN YOU'RE A TEEN AND BOYS START CALLING...

FAIRY TALE

Top Tip: *You can't lock your child up for ever, so prepare them for life in advance.*

'That Talk'

So how *do* we provide our children with that internal 'chastity belt'? Part of the answer is simply to swallow hard, put your embarrassment behind you and talk to them about the big 'S' word. Don't worry, you're not odd. No mum or dad has ever talked to their teenager about sex without finding it a struggle at first just to get the words out – which, of course, is why so many parents put the whole thing off until it's too late to be of any use. But no matter how shy or embarrassed we are, poll after poll shows that teenagers want to learn about sex initially from their parents, rather than from friends, magazines, the TV or even their school.

So however difficult it is, it's vital to learn to discuss this important issue within the home, and – though it's probably a bit too late to say this – to start early. If you *don't* talk to your child about sex, it only leaves the door open for their imaginations to run riot, filled with myths and half-truths picked up from elsewhere.

I learnt the facts of life from my mate John Dean when I was ten. And that was a long time ago. These days, sex is out in the open and used to sell everything from magazines to ice cream. We're all exposed to a bombardment of sexual images every day, both blatant and concealed. No child over the age of seven or eight can escape constant talk of sex, though what they actually pick up at this age is bound to be a mixture of half-truths and misunderstandings. The problem is that, without your involvement, there's no guarantee that these won't persist well into their teenage years.

Top Tip: *Your teenager wants to hear about sex from* **you** *first.*

Little and Often

Once relegated to the biology classroom, sex education has now been 'upgraded' to the National Curriculum: this means that most schools teach something of the emotional and social aspects of sex as well as a guide to 'what goes where'. But don't be tempted to think that lets you off the hook.

For one thing, nothing taught about sex at school is going to be 'value-free': something of the teacher's own moral opinions will inevitably creep into their lessons, however hard they try to be objective. There's no guarantee you'll agree with them, so it's important for you to present your own values alongside those your teenager will come into contact with at school, in the media and from their friends.

But that's not the only reason why they need to talk about sex with you. There are bound to be things *you* can explain to your teenager that they *won't* learn in school. Few teenagers are brave enough to risk parading their ignorance or misunderstandings in front of their friends by asking too many questions – even if everyone else secretly wants to know the answers as well!

The easiest way to start talking about sex is to introduce the subject gently and naturally as your child first starts asking about where they came from. If you save the whole thing up for the mammoth sixteen-hour 'Big Talk' lecture session when they're thirteen or fourteen, they'll simply squirm with embarrassment for the first half hour and fall asleep for the rest. But just as importantly, they won't understand that sex is a natural part of life. By now, of course, it's too late to say this. But don't despair, because the same basic principle applies, however late you've left it.

It's better to talk to your teenager about sex 'little and often' than all at once. It gives them time to think things through. What's more, it's actually less embarrassing for both of you, especially if you choose your moments carefully. And of course, this means you don't need to be artificial in the way you broach things – you're never far away from an opportunity to talk to your son or daughter about some aspect of sex or sexuality, because some aspect of sex and sexuality is never far away. But don't fall into the trap of *over-doing it*, raising the subject with boring regularity at every possible opportunity – if you do, they'll switch off and reach the obvious conclusion that you're obsessed.

Top Tip: *Talk to your teenager about sex little and often, not all at once.*

Under Pressure

Some parents are worried that teaching their children about sex will push them into sexual relationships too soon. So not wanting to 'shatter their innocence', they choose to keep silent. But this is a potentially disastrous plan. The World Health Organisation reports that not only is there *no* evidence that sex education leads to more or earlier sexual activity, all the research suggests that exactly the opposite is true: good sex education tends to push *up* the age at which teenagers have sex, not bring it *down*.

As the saying goes, 'forewarned is forearmed'. Being armed with enough information usually delays a child's sexual activity. The truth is that *innocence* is more likely to be protected when *ignorance* is removed. Your openness and honesty will help your teenager to make better, more informed, more mature and more responsible choices in the face of considerable pressure from their hormones, their friends and the media.

According to the Family Planning Association, most of the 8,000 under-sixteens who become pregnant in the UK every year weren't even looking to have sex, let alone a baby. They just got carried away. In other words, they had sex without really deciding to. And the main reason why they allowed themselves to be swept along in the heat of passion? 'I just didn't know how to say no.'

When teenagers hit puberty, their hormones suddenly explode. Filled with emotions and impulses they've not experienced before, and usually convinced that they're the only people ever to have felt them so intensely, they're under huge pressure. Having emerged from an age at which any physical contact with the opposite sex seemed even less appealing than eating a slug sandwich, they now find themselves coming to terms with impulses and urges that are as bewildering as they are exciting. From *never* having really thought about sex, they suddenly find themselves *always* thinking about sex.

But teenagers are also under pressure to conform with their peers, amongst whom sexual activity often becomes a badge of honour. In fact, having had sex can assume almost mythical proportions. The pressure to do what you think all your friends are doing is intense – even when it turns out later that most of them *aren't* actually doing it at all! In fact, only one in four boys and one in five girls has sex before the age of sixteen, though most fifteen-year-olds are led to feel like the only virgin left on the face of the earth.

Most teenagers desperately need to feel loved and accepted, especially by their peers. We're told that 80 per cent of teenagers are unhappy with their looks: their nose, hair, height, weight, glasses, zits – or, in some cases, the whole lot! Sex can offer them reassurance that they're attractive and desirable.

On top of all this, young people live in a society that teaches them they should behave like adults. And to teenagers, the most important part of being an adult is – sex. The adult world appears obsessed with sex, so our expectations for them to behave like adults can ironically push them into experimenting with or having sex before they feel ready. To them, sex can seem to be *the* short cut to instant adulthood.

Top Tip: Help your teenager resist sexual pressure – forewarned is forearmed.

Thou Shalt Not?

A friend of mine says that the first time anyone told him about sex, back in the 1950s, they gave him some advice he'll never forget: 'Sex is dirty,' they said. 'It's degrading and disgusting. Save it for your wife!' Though he can laugh about it now, he admits that this pathetic explanation left him confused for a long time. Another friend says that her mother often still tells her, 'I want you to know I'm proud I was "clean" until I married your father!'

It's not enough to tell your kids what they *shouldn't* do when it comes to sex. If you don't give them a *positive*, healthy approach to sex and sexuality, you risk leaving them unprepared for what's ahead. And if you don't teach them how to cope with their emotions, you'll risk exposing them to lots of unnecessary pain and heartache later on.

If you don't present sex as being, in the right circumstances, something not just wholesome but wonderful, your teenager may well grow up imagining it's shameful and sordid. As a result, not only will they probably not get the best out of it, they may even feel guilty about enjoying it. And that's not just unfortunate: it's potentially disastrous.

Two centuries ago, before the French Revolution, Pierre Choderlos de Laclos wrote a book called *Dangerous Liaisons* that inflamed and outraged polite society. It tells the story of a teenager, fresh out of convent school, whose sex education has been all about *don'ts* rather than *dos*. Totally unprepared for the passion and strength of her feelings and desires, she can't see how something she was taught was a 'necessary evil' – to be endured for the good of the species, but never enjoyed – could feel so good. As a result, she's an easy target for a young aristocrat who seduces her, then discards her as soon as he's got what he wants. Times may have changed but human nature hasn't, and thousands of people face exactly the same problems today.

The truth is, *sexuality* is about a lot more than just sex. It's about being human. Sexuality is part of who we are. So what we teach teenagers about sex and sexuality is what we teach them about life, and about being human. If we leave them with the impression that there's something inherently wrong with sex, we'll leave them feeling that there's something wrong with them and their feelings.

Sooner or later, your son or daughter will make their own choices about when, where and with whom they have sex. If you want these choices to be informed and responsible, you need to teach them and talk to them about sex in a positive, natural and guilt-free way.

Top Tip: *Be positive – remember that sex is nothing to be ashamed of!*

115

The Moment of Truth

But what happens when it actually comes to the crunch? You've given your teenager all the advice you can. You've prepared them as far as possible to choose wisely when it comes to boyfriends or girlfriends. But now they've got one, and you don't approve of their choice. What now?

The first thing to remember is that it's *their* choice and *their* relationship – whether you approve or not. So don't assume you've necessarily got to like everyone your child goes out with, or enthusiastically endorse a relationship just because it exists. When your teenager asks what you think – which they'll do eventually, if you're at all close – tell them about your concerns. But try to express your reservations as sensitively as you can, whilst at the same time making it clear that you have an open mind, and that your only motive is for them to be secure and happy.

Remember: your teenager's choice of boyfriend or girlfriend says something about their own personality. So if you set your sights on actively trying to drive them apart and bringing the relationship to an end, your plan may well backfire, with the result that you end up pushing them together whilst simultaneously driving a wedge between them and *you*! What's more, if you're wrong, and the relationship turns out to be a healthy and long-term one, you'll have a huge mountain to climb in order to restore the trust between you. And even if you turn out to be right, you'll still have put a barrier between you and your child that could seriously hamper your relationship for years to come. If they get the impression you don't trust their judgment, and come to resent your interference, you may well discover to your cost that you have less influence over their decisions than ever.

James and Cathy were delighted when their nineteen-year-old daughter, Fiona, told them she was getting married. Though she was young to be taking such a big step, they knew how mature and level-headed she was, and looked forward to meeting their future son-in-law. But when they finally did, they both instinctively felt he wasn't the right man for her. For a start, he was a lot older. Things got worse and worse, until they finally told her they wouldn't have anything to do with her wedding. When their son, Mark, tried to persuade them to change their minds, they were adamant: 'We're only thinking of what's best for her. The marriage will never work. It'll all end in tears.' 'If you don't support her, you'll lose her,' Mark replied. 'If you're right, and the marriage falls apart, you won't be there to pick up the pieces. But if you're wrong, and it works, you'll never see her again. Or your grandchildren. You *have* to support her, even if you think she's wrong. What have you got to lose that could possibly mean more than your daughter?'

My friend Gerald has a simple rule: 'Never write people off.' If your son or daughter comes home with someone you think is completely unsuitable, take another look. Try to see what *they* find attractive about them. If there really *isn't* anything, at least you'll still be on speaking terms with your child when they finally work it out for themselves!

 Top Tip: Be supportive of your teenager, especially when they make mistakes.

House Rules

If you think your teenager is making a mistake in their choice of partner, or slipping into a sexually active relationship before they're ready, try not to explode or start laying down the law too heavily. For someone in their teens, being ordered by a parent *not* to do something is usually the single best reason for doing it.

However, you *can* and should set limits on what they do or don't do, both in your own house and elsewhere. Part of your role as a parent is to draw the moral boundaries for this, as for every other area of their life – they still need a clear steer from you about what's right and wrong. Just allowing a teenager to do what they like when they like is *not* the mark of a loving parent. If you don't help them to make wise and responsible sexual choices, they or someone else could get hurt. They may resent the limits, and even push against them, but they need them to be there for their protection. Like the legal age of consent, your rules may not stop your teenager from entering or continuing an unhelpful relationship, but they'll give them a clear idea what *you* think is acceptable behaviour, and what boundaries you expect them to honour.

Of course, none of this means you will necessarily be able to stop your teenager from making mistakes or doing things you think they shouldn't. But at the same time, it's part of your responsibility as a parent to give a moral lead, or they'll reach the conclusion either that you approve of what they're doing – which will probably confuse them, especially if they're not 100 per cent convinced it's the right thing themselves – or else that you don't care what they do, and whether or not they get hurt.

MY PARENTS SET CLEAR BOUNDARIES...

MINE TOO. BUT I THINK THE ELECTRIC FENCE IS A BIT HARSH.

Most teenagers have seen a few '18 Certificate' films by the time they're actually eighteen. I suspect our kids will be no exception. Nevertheless, we have a rule in our house that no one can watch a film they're not legally entitled to watch. It may not stop them from seeing an '18' film at a friend's house – though we hope it'll at least make them think twice – but we want them to realise that the censorship rules are there for a reason, and we don't approve of breaking them.

You've got to give your teenager freedom, but you've also got to ensure as best you can that that freedom is exercised within safe limits. So work out in advance what kind of sexual standards and boundaries you expect them to hold to, and make sure they know that's what you expect, and why.

If they break the rules, instead of flying off the handle, try to let them know why you're disappointed with them, and reaffirm what the boundaries are. Any punishment you hand out should be aimed at reinforcing the rule – the 'safety limit' – and re-emphasising why it was there, not just letting them know how angry you are that they broke it.

At the end of the day, it's your responsibility to do all you can to help your teenager make good sexual choices – ones they won't regret in the morning, or even five or ten years down the line – but you can't make their choices for them. You can't *control* what they do, only act as a *guide*, helping them work out for themselves what kind of sexual behaviour is healthy, acceptable and likely to make them happier in the long run.

Top Tip: *Work out how you want your teenager to behave, and clearly communicate your boundaries and your reasons.*

You Have Nothing to Lose but Your Apron Strings

How Do I Let My Teenager Go?

Jason lives alone. Every morning he catches the train to his job in the City, and every evening he comes back to his little suburban flat. The routine never varies. He never goes out, and never has friends over for dinner. He's summed up in a line from the John Mellencamp song, 'Jack and Diane': 'Life goes on, long after the thrill of living is gone.'

There's nothing physically wrong with Jason. It's just that he has no self-confidence or social skills. And the reason for this is simple: his father died when he was young but his mother, who died about ten years ago, mollycoddled and smothered him well into his forties. He never freed himself of her apron strings.

And because she'd overprotected him, he didn't know what to do or how to cope after she died. Jason's afraid of anything that doesn't fit his set routine, simply because his mum's love for him made her tragically blind to the fact that she was failing to prepare him for independent living. He can cook and use a washing machine, but he doesn't know how to make friends or take decisions. Instead of being the master of his own destiny, he's at the mercy of the future.

There was once a scientific study done into how people react to meeting someone with a facial disfigurement. An actress was hired to do a bogus survey in a shopping centre, and the whole thing was secretly filmed from a nearby shop. She was asked to do the same survey in four different 'roles'. *First* she had to be herself. *Then* she had to act awkwardly, without any self-confidence. *Third*, she was made up to look as though she had a very off-putting birthmark on her face. And *finally*, with the same birthmark make-up, she again had to act awkwardly, with no self-confidence.

The results surprised even the scientists doing the experiment. The birthmark *did* make people slightly nervous, but it was the actress's charm and self-confidence, or lack of them, that actually made all the difference. They proved to be a far bigger factor than her looks. The team responsible for the study concluded that people with enough self-confidence and self-esteem, and an ability to make friends, can overcome even the most severe disability. But people without these social skills – like Jason – have a disadvantage in life that has a far more negative impact than any physical disability.

So if you want your child to be truly happy and successful, you need to prepare them for what's ahead by working to develop in them the self-confidence, self-esteem, self-discipline and self-worth that are *all* vital if they're to be able to cope well with life. Beyond any shadow of doubt, it's preparation, not protection, that's the key.

 Top Tip: *If you don't prepare your teenager for life on their own, they'll never be ready.*

Be Prepared!

In the film *Who Framed Roger Rabbit?* Roger is left in charge of baby Herman while Herman's mum is out. Safe in his playpen, Herman seems a babysitter's dream – even for a cartoon rabbit. But then everything goes wrong.

Because of Roger's stupidity, Herman escapes from his cage and crawls to the kitchen in search of cookies. What follows is every mother's worst nightmare. He only narrowly avoids being skewered in the cutlery drawer, burnt alive on the cooker, drowned in the sink, cut to pieces by kitchen knives, and splatted all over the floor when he falls off the fridge.

While Herman was in his playpen, he was safe. But once he'd left its confines, life suddenly became extremely dangerous. And it's the same in real life. Mums and dads naturally want to protect their children from the horrors of the outside world, filled with all sorts of perils and dangers. Obviously, the safest thing to do is to shut the front door and keep them warm and secure, locked up at home.

But even if doing this were possible, it would be as short-sighted and ineffective as King Canute's attempt to turn back the tide. Although Canute was a great and powerful king, there was no way he was ever going to be able to stop the tide from coming in.

One day, your teenager will leave home. They'll live on their own or with friends. They'll struggle to survive on too little money. They'll walk home down long, dark streets late at night. They'll choose their own friends and partners, and do what they like with them. They'll drive cars or ride motorbikes, go to parties and raves. They'll choose their own clothes, deciding for themselves whether or not to wear a coat, hat, scarf and mittens. Like it or not, your control over them will be gone.

But how well they'll cope with being on their own, making all of their own decisions, is largely up to you. It's your task to begin work *now* to prepare them for the moment they leave home.

Top Tip: *You can't keep your teenager locked up at home for the rest of their life, so* **preparation** *is the key.*

Branching Out

Your 'mission impossible', whether you actually choose to accept it or not, is to teach your child how to handle themselves safely and responsibly whilst they're still inside the protective confines of the 'playpen'. It may not always seem like it, but teenagers haven't left the 'playpen' yet. They still need a perimeter fence, marking the safe limits beyond which it's dangerous to go, but within which they can enjoy their freedom.

This perimeter fence is a vital part of your responsibility to protect your kids from harm, teaching them right from wrong. Allowing a teenager to do what they like when they like is *not* the hallmark of a loving parent. If you don't teach them to behave in a responsible way – in everything from their bedtimes and homework to their relationships and honesty – you're only storing up trouble for them further down the line. Not only will they lack the self-discipline they need to make the best and most fulfilling use of their own time and talents, but eventually, if they don't learn to be kind and considerate with other people, they'll come up against someone who'll be only too happy to 'teach them a lesson they'll never forget'.

Your teenager will, of course, inevitably push against this fence. But at the same time, they rely on it being there to protect them. Like the walls of a playpen, the rules you give your teenager must provide them both with *freedom* and *safe limits*, because they'll need *both* if they're to grow up to become constructive and responsible members of society. If you don't give your teenager safe limits, they'll hurt themselves. But if you don't give them enough freedom, they'll eventually take it anyway. One day they'll do just as they please. If you haven't prepared them enough, they won't have had enough experience of freedom to know how to handle it wisely, and they'll suffer as a result.

ONE OF THE HOUSE RULES IS YOU DON'T INTERRUPT MUM WHEN SHE'S WATCHING HER YOGA VIDEO.

YES—BUT SHE'S FLEXIBLE ON THAT ONE.

So the goal in your child's teenage years isn't to abandon the 'playpen' altogether, but gradually to enlarge it, because as they grow and develop, children need, and are able to handle, greater and greater levels of freedom and choice. Previous, tighter limits on what they were allowed to do will have taught them to handle this freedom wisely.

Your task is gradually to allow rules to give way to freedom and trust. (For example, from setting strict bedtimes when they're twelve or thirteen, you can slowly let them determine their own bedtimes, so they can learn to judge how to balance their need for sleep with their desire to enjoy themselves.) That way, when they can finally break down the perimeter fences altogether, they will appreciate and enjoy living in a way that both respects and protects others as well as themselves.

It's all a bit like when you teach a child to ride a two-wheeler. You start by promising not to let go of the saddle, and run alongside them as they get the feel of it. Then, when they're confident enough, you do let go – but only for a second or two. Eventually, when they're able to go short distances on their own, you let go for longer periods, still running alongside just in case. In the end, they can manage perfectly well without you.

 Top Tip: By slowly making your house rules more flexible, you give your teenager both **freedom** and **safe limits**.

Going by the Rules

Getting the balance right, and slowly allowing your child to replace *your* rules with *their* judgment as they get older, is one of the most difficult challenges any parent faces. Some rules and boundaries – 'Don't cross the road on your own', for instance – obviously come with built-in 'sell-by' dates. But unfortunately there's no chart available setting out the precise schedule for the move from strict rules to greater freedom and trust. Each teenager is unique: they handle responsibility in their own way and in their own time, which means that once again it's the quantity and quality of time you invest in getting to know your teenager that will be your best guide.

In our house, for example, there's a sharp division between boys and girls when it comes to setting bedtimes. Our two daughters, sixteen-year-old Emily and twelve-year-old Abigail, announce that they're off to bed when they're tired. It's been that way for years. But when it comes to our boys, it's a whole different matter. Fourteen-year-old Daniel and ten-year-old Josh would never go to bed without being pointed in the right direction. If we left it up to them, they'd stay up all night. They'd wake up in the morning still in yesterday's clothes, dog tired and with a crick in their necks from having fallen asleep in front of the television. Their work would suffer – and so would their looks!

The parent who's looking for a list of *dos* and *don'ts*, and a firm timetable for letting go, is the kind of parent who'd make mistakes even if such timetables were available. In order to work out when to keep your teenager on a tight lead and when to let go, you need to spend lots of time getting to know them. There's no alternative or short cut to this. You've got to make time to get to know their wants and needs, their strengths and weaknesses, and their unique ways of seeing the world. If you don't, you'll simply end up reacting to their behaviour in a non-constructive way rather than thoughtfully working to shape it with them.

Top Tip: *You've got to know your teenager well to know how flexible to be with your house rules.*

Viva Democracy!

The older your child gets, the more involved they can – and *should* – be in shaping the rules that govern their behaviour: when they go to bed, when they can go out and with whom, what they should wear, etc.

Though your family isn't a democracy – you're the boss! – by acting as if it *were* a lot of the time you can help train your child to take responsibility for their own life. If they feel they 'own' the rules, they'll be less likely to break them and more inclined to accept the penalties when they do. What's more, involving them in creating the rules sends them the message that you respect them, and that's the biggest motivator they can have to respect *you* by keeping the rules.

But remember, they'll find it difficult to agree to rules that don't make any sense to them. So you'll need to think carefully through what your regulations are, and why they exist, before you sit down with your teenager to set them. The more sensible they seem, the more likely they are to be accepted.

And watch out: the rules you make are likely to include checks on *your* behaviour as well! Like it or not, you undermine both your rules and your authority whenever you violate them or unreasonably claim they don't apply to you. It confuses kids when adults seem to play by a whole different set of rules. If you make a law that doesn't apply to you, you'll need to explain clearly and convincingly *why* you're exempt. The more fair and reasonable your total package of rules is, the easier this task will be.

Top Tip: *The more involved your teenager is in making the rules in the first place, the more likely they are to keep them.*

Delegation – That's What You Need!

The art of delegation is the art of knowing when to move from strict sets of rules to ever greater degrees of trust and responsibility. And the better you know your child, the more able you are to make good judgments about how and when to do this. Too much responsibility too soon can be totally overwhelming, but too little too late will always leave them believing you don't trust them.

Self-confidence and self-discipline develop as you slowly grant your child greater and greater levels of responsibility, and the freedom that goes with it. This is the best way a parent has of saying, 'I trust you'. If you don't do this, your child will never *feel* trusted or trustworthy. And that means they're unlikely to *become* trustworthy.

Pocket money is a good example of delegation, because it allows you to give your teenager some of the responsibility for buying the things they want or need. By granting them limited control over their finances, you begin to teach them the budgeting skills they'll need later in life. What's more, giving your teenager a budget to choose and buy their own clothes and accessories – not just their own games, vidoes, CDs, etc. – is a further way of creating trust and helping them learn to handle money wisely.

Our oldest three children all have bank accounts, complete with cash cards and, once they're old enough, cheque books. (At ten, Joshua's too young to be allowed a proper bank account.) Abigail and Daniel get their pocket money paid straight in, but Emily's on a monthly allowance. Cornie and I have calculated roughly what we spend per month on her clothes, entertainment, etc., and have arranged for that money to be paid directly into her account. Now it's up to her how she manages it, though of course we're still there to give advice if she needs it. We've also helped all three to set up standing orders to the charity of their choice, so they get used to money regularly flowing *out* of their account as well as going *into* it.

It's vital to understand that delegation of any kind is *never* about washing your hands of responsibility. Some people see it as a way of passing the buck. But that's not delegation – it's dumping! In my job, I delegate huge amounts of work. But this doesn't mean

I'm no longer responsible for it. Though the actual work is entrusted to others, it's still up to me to ensure they're getting the backup, support and guidance they need. If things are going badly, it's just as much my fault as anyone else's. Delegation is about *sharing* responsibility with others, not dumping it on them. *They* are responsible for the details, but you are responsible for *them*. If they have too much responsibility to handle, or too little to inspire them, you haven't delegated well.

 Top Tip: *The more responsibility a teenager is given, the more responsibly they'll behave.*

If at First You Don't Succeed ...

Delegation can, of course, be extremely frustrating. When you first teach someone to do something, there are bound to be 'teething problems'. Mistakes are inevitable when anyone learns something new. It's at this point that you face the temptation to take the reins back and do it yourself. But trusting someone with a task and then taking it away again is like saying that you've realised they're not trustworthy, and the end result will be worse than what you started with. So rather than blaming them and giving up when things are going wrong, you need to tweak the system a little bit by adjusting the level of responsibility given.

So practise the five steps to effective delegation:

1 know your teenager well;
2 think about the appropriate level of responsibility to delegate to them;
3 keep your cool when problems inevitably occur;
4 encourage them by pointing out what they do *right*; and
5 urge them to try again when they fail.

And remember: you're still ultimately responsible for all the things you delegate to your teenager, which means keeping a constant check on how they're getting on. However, the art is to be careful not to make your involvement sound like an interrogation. If you do, you'll soon discover than an exercise originally designed to inspire confidence and trust will end up undermining it. But as you get it right, your teenager will grow in the confidence, expertise and – because they feel *trusted – trustworthiness* they'll need for the future.

One day your teenager will leave home – whether they're ready for it or not. That means preparation is the key. So grasp the opportunity you have to prepare them *now*! If you want your teenager to be an adult you're proud of tomorrow, make sure you're an adult they can be proud of today.

Top Tip: *Delegation isn't dumping, so make sure your teenager still has all the advice and support they need.*

THE LAST WORD

The Navajo Indians of North America incorporate a kind of 'Marriage Race' into every wedding, as I found out a few years ago when I went to one. As part of the ceremony, all the women in the village run around its boundaries with the new bride. The bride finishes this 'race' first, with her immediate family – her mother, aunts and sisters – close behind, and all the other women just behind them. This isn't a tradition designed to ensure that all the women of the village get regular exercise. It's a powerful symbol of the way the Navajo recognise that we all need ongoing support from the whole community.

There was a time when you'd have known just where to turn for help in our society too. Uncles, aunts, parents, grandparents and great-grandparents all lived in the same village. They were on hand to offer useful and relevant guidance, support and babysitting when you needed it. But the family has shrunk considerably in the last century. Fifty years ago, your mother lived in the same street. A hundred years ago, she lived in the same house. Now you're lucky if she even lives in the same part of the country. Smaller families have given us independence, but at what cost? As extended families grow apart, we're becoming more and more isolated. Entire communities used to play a part in raising every child. Now we often feel as though we're out on our own, left to fend for ourselves.

But the truth is, you're *not* alone. Beyond this book, there are all sorts of resources available in the difficult, but rewarding, task of being a parent. From books and videos to courses and specialist organisations, help is literally only a phone call away. The next few pages give just an example of the kind of resources on offer, but for more information you can write to **Parentalk** at:

PO Box 23142, London, SE1 0ZT

Whatever you do, *don't* try to go it alone. You can be a great parent, so if you need help, get in touch.

FURTHER INFORMATION

Organisations

Parentalk
PO Box 23142
London SE1 0ZT

Tel: 0700 2000 500
Fax: 020 7450 9060
e-mail: info@parentalk.co.uk
Website: http://www.parentalk.co.uk

*Provides a range of resources and
services designed to inspire parents
to enjoy parenthood.*

Positive Parenting Publications
1st floor
2A South Street
Gosport PO12 1ES

Tel: 023 9252 8787
Fax: 023 9520 1111
e-mail: info@parenting.org.uk
Website: http://
          www.parenting.org.uk

*Aims to prepare people for the role
of parenting by helping parents,
those about to become parents and
also those who lead parenting groups.*

Gingerbread
16–17 Clerkenwell Close
London
EC1R 0AA

Advice line:
          0800 018 4314
e-mail: office@gingerbread.org.uk
Website: http://
          www.gingerbread.org.uk

*Provides day-to-day support and
practical help for lone parents.*

Parentline Plus
520 Highgate Studios
53–76 Highgate Road
Kentish Town
London
NW5 1TL

Helpline: 0808 800 2222
Fax: 020 7284 5501
e-mail: centraloffice@
          parentlineplus.org.uk
Website: http://
www.parentlineplus.org.uk

*Provides freephone helpline called
Parentline and courses for parents
via the Parent Network Service.
Parentline Plus also includes the
National Stepfamily Association.
For all information call the
Parentline freephone number on
0808 800 2222*

NSPCC
42 Curtain Road
London EC2A 3NH

Helpline: 0800 800 500
Tel: 020 7825 2500
Fax: 020 7825 2525
Website: http://www.nspcc.org.uk

*Aims to prevent child abuse and
neglect in all its forms and give
practical help to families with
children at risk.*

Care for the Family
Garth House
Leon Avenue
Cardiff CF4 7RG

Tel: 029 2081 1733
Fax: 029 2081 4089
e-mail: mail@cff.org.uk
Web site: http://
www.care-for-the-family.org.uk

*Providing support for families
through seminars, resources and
special projects.*

Kidscape
2 Grovesnor Gardens
London SW1W 0DH

Tel: 020 7730 3300
Fax: 020 7730 7081
e-mail: info@kidscape.org.uk
Website: http://www.kidscape.org.uk

*Works to prevent the abuse of
children through education
programmes involving parents and
teachers, providing a range of
resources. Also runs a bullying
helpline.*

YouthNet UK

e-mail: youthnet@thesite.org.uk
Website: http://www.thesite.org.uk

*Aims to give young people access
via the Internet to the most
comprehensive information
available.*

National Drugs Helpline
0800 77 66 00
Healthwise Helplines Limited
First Floor
Cavern Court
8 Matthew Street
Liverpool L2 6RE

*Free helpline offering confidential
advice. Can also send out free
leaflets and answer any questions
callers might have.*

Publications

The Sixty Minute Father, Rob Parsons, Hodder and Stoughton
How to Succeed as a Parent, Steve Chalke, Hodder and Stoughton
Sex Matters, Steve Chalke, Hodder and Stoughton
Positive Parenting: Raising Children with Self Esteem, E. Hartley-Brewer,
    Mandarin Paperback
Raising Boys, Steve Biddulph, Thorsons
The Secret of Happy Children, Steve Biddulph, Thorsons
Families and How to Survive Them, Skinner and Cleese, Vermilion
Stress Free Parenting, Dr David Haslam, Vermilion
How Not to be a Perfect Mother, Libby Purves, Harper Collins

Parenting Courses

• **Parentalk Parenting Course**
A new parenting course designed to give parents the opportunity to share
their experiences, learn from each other and discover some principles of
parenting.

Parentalk
PO Box 23142, London SE1 0ZT

• **Parent Network**
Operates through self-help groups run by parents for parents known as
Parent-Link. The groups are mostly run for 2 or more hours, over 13 weekly
sessions.

For more information call **Parentline Plus** on 080 800 2222

• **Positive Parenting Publications**
Publish a range of low cost, easy to read, common sense resource materials
which provide help, information and advice. Responsible for running a range
of parenting courses across the UK.

For more information phone 023 9252 8787

The **Paren**talk Parenting Course

Helping you to be a Better Parent

Being a parent is not easy. **Parentalk** is a new, video-led, parenting course designed to give groups of parents the opportunity to share their experiences, learn from each other and discover some principles of parenting. It is suitable for anyone who is a parent or is planning to become a parent.

The Parentalk Parenting Course features:

Steve Chalke – TV Presenter; author on parenting and family issues; father of four and **Parentalk** Founder.
Rob Parsons – author of *The Sixty Minute Father*; regular TV and radio contributor; and Executive Director of Care for the Family.
Dr Caroline Dickinson – inner city-based GP and specialist in obstetrics, gynaecology and paediatrics.
Kate Robbins – well known actress and comedienne.

Each **Parentalk** session is packed with group activities and discussion starters.

Made up of eight sessions, the **Parentalk** Parenting Course is easy to use and includes everything you need to host a group of up to ten parents.

Each Parentalk Course Pack contains:
• A **Parentalk** Video
• Extensive, easy to use, group leader's guide
• Ten copies of the full-colour course material for members
• Photocopiable sheets/OHP masters

Price £49.95

Additional participant materials are available so that the course can be run again and again.

To order your copy, or to find out more, please contact:

Parentalk

PO Box 23142, London SE1 0ZT
Tel: 020 7450 9072 or 020 7450 9073
Fax: 020 7450 9060
e-Mail: info@parentalk.co.uk